ANARCHY IN THE UK
THE STORIES BEHIND THE ANTHEMS OF
PUNK

STEVEN WELLS

Acknowledgements

I would like to thank Alex Burrows for his help and assistance with the writing and research of this book.

Steven Wells

This is a Carlton book

First published by in Great Britain in 2003 by Carlton Books Limited
20 Mortimer Street
London W1T 3JW

Text copyright and design copyright © Carlton Books 2004

ISBN 1 84442 823 0

Project Editor: Lorna Russell
Picture research: Elena Goodison
Art Director: Lucy Coley
Design:Barbara Zuñiga
Cover design: Alison Tutton
Production: Lisa Moore

CONTENTS

"Punk was an international outsider aesthetic: dark, tribal, alienated, full of black humour. It spread from the US through the UK and France and through Europe, Japan and Australia during the years following 1975. For anyone...who felt cast out because of class, sexuality, perception, gender, even choice, who felt useless, unworthy, ashamed...(punk was) an attraction/repulsion machine of...infernal power that offered the chance of action, even surrender – to something larger than you – and thus possible transcendence. In becoming a nightmare, you could find your dreams."

Jon Savage, *England's Dreaming – Sex Pistols and Punk Rock*

Introduction

Punk was the most exciting thing ever to happen to music. And not just music. It changed everything from fine art to fashion. What started as an obnoxious noise made by a bunch of scrawny social misfits mushroomed into a worldwide phenomenon that touched the lives of millions.

The argument still rages – who invented punk? The Brits or the Yanks? Let's settle that once and for all.

Punk started in America. But it exploded in Britain.

Before the Sex Pistols, punk was an underground scene. After the Sex Pistols, punk infected the world.

Punk was a musical revolution. Before punk, rock music was dominated by long-haired, self-indulgent millionaires. Bands composed of incredibly skilled musicians bored audiences rigid with tedious concept albums and wanky guitar solos. Punk blew all that away. It said that ANYBODY could be a musician. The punk fanzine *Sniffin' Glue* printed a diagram of three guitar chords accompanied by the caption: "This is a chord. This is another. This is a third. NOW FORM A BAND."

So people did – and it really was that simple.

The American writer Greil Marcus defined punk as "refusing the future society has planned for you". And the amazing thing is that thousands of kids did exactly that. They became singers, guitarists, drummers, writers, publishers, designers, promoters, poets – and all without anybody's permission.

Punk burst out of the art school and onto the streets. And things went seriously mental. Suddenly there were thousands of bands pumping out thousands of self-financed singles. The major record companies scrambled furiously to sign anybody who could hold a guitar and sneer at the same time.

Punk was rock's Year Zero. It was forward to basics. It was about imagination and enthusiasm being far more important than talent or money or looks. It was the geeks' revenge. It was the nerds' nirvana. The girls dressed like whores and the boys looked like rent boys.

For many, the Sex Pistols define the era.

Outraged bigots attacked kids in the streets. Concerts were cancelled, records were blacklisted, bands were banned and politicians, priests and newspaper pundits screamed for punk to be stamped out.

There were riots, there were screaming tabloid headlines, there were questions asked in Parliament. There were communist punks, anarchist punks, socialist punks, gay-rights punks and feminist punks (and even a few totally deluded idiot nazi punks). And this wasn't just happening "underground" – it was seeping into and mutating the mainstream. The Sex Pistols got to Number 1 in the British charts with the sneering "God Save The Queen" in the very week of Her Majesty's Royal Jubilee. To the British establishment, it was as if their own children had suddenly turned into screaming demons from hell.

Rock'n'roll hadn't been this exciting since the 1950s. The adult world recoiled in revulsion. The media sold the punks as modern folk devils – as the filthy, depraved, swearing, spitting scum of the earth.

They weren't, of course. They were just kids having the time of their lives – and making and listening to fantastic music while they did so.

But punk was more than that just rock music. It was more than just another cult. More than just another fad. More than just another musical genre for the record companies to sanitize, shrink-wrap and sell to the ignorant masses. Punk was also the last great artistic movement of the 20th century – the successor to Dadaism and surrealism. But, unlike most artistic movements, punk wasn't the property of a few gifted artists. It had (and has) a cast of millions.

And when punk in the UK did finally fizzle out, it exploded again in the US in the shape of hardcore. And it's never really gone away since. Every generation that has followed has felt the need to make a godawful, angry row. And whether they do it with drums and guitars or with synthesizers and sequencers, it's still punk.

Today, of course, there are plenty of powder-puff McPunks around peddling an MTV-friendly "lite" version of the real thing. But there are also plenty of genuine punks around, too. And they're easy to spot – they're the ones with the soul, the passion and the power.

And they're the ones making the great music.

Why writing this book was a nightmare

Aaaargh! Where do you start? Where do you finish?

And that's the problem. For a book like this, do you include those '60s garage "punk" bands? How about Nirvana and the rest of the grungers? What about the "new wave" acts like Elvis Costello, Wreckless Eric and Ian Dury? Are they punk? How about Busted and Blink 182 and Good Charlotte?

While researching this book I asked 20 people for their top 10 punk songs. No two lists were the same. But they all included songs by The Clash and the Sex Pistols. And most of them agreed that no list would be complete without Iggy Pop And The Stooges, Johnny Thunders and The Ramones.

But that's when you hit your next problem. The US hardcore punk bands of the 1980s obviously belong in these pages. But who else? Where do you stop?

Nirvana were obviously a punk band. As were Rage Against The Machine. But do they belong in this book? Probably not. But what about the '90s Riot Grrl bands like Bikini Kill and Huggy Bear? Er...and what about the "new wave of new wave" bands like S*M*A*S*H and Elastica and These Animal Men? Um...were the Au Pairs a punk band? What about The Three Johns? Why no mention of Pansy Division? Why isn't Amen's brilliant "Piss Virus" in here? What about Joey Ramone's solo stuff? How come you've not mentioned any Italian, French, Finnish, Dutch, Brazilian, Mexican or Spanish bands? What about Billy Bragg? Weren't The Prodigy punk? And Napalm Death? And Fugazi? And Chicks On Speed? And Alec Empire? And the Manic Street Preachers?

Why are there no early Jam songs? What about Oi? Or Action Pact? Or Scritti Politti? Or punk poet John Cooper Clarke? Or the Young Marble Giants? Or Johnny Moped? Or Nation Of Ulysses? Or The Parkinsons? Or Ed Banger And The Nosebleeds? Or Jon The Postman? Or Prag Vec? What about "Kung Fu" by Ash? Or "Baby Sitter" by the Stupid Babies? Or The Quads' brilliant "There Must Be Thousands"? Or Splodgenessabounds'

seminal "Two Pints Of Lager And A Packet Of Crisps Please"? Or...

AAAAAARGH!

OK, so here's what I've done. I've concentrated mainly on '70s punk and '80s hardcore. And mainly on UK and US bands. And mainly on the records that had the most impact and changed the most lives. And then I've cheated. I've stuck in some songs – like Jilted John's "Jilted John", Plastic Bertrand's "Ça Plane Pour Moi" and Shampoo's "Trouble" – that'll have the anal retentive nitpicking purist types screaming with outrage. Sod them. Punk was just as much about taking the piss as it was about smashing the system. And besides, they still make me hoot with joy.

I've included a few relatively obscure songs – like The Newtown Neurotics' "Kick Out The Tories" – just because they're so damn good. And I've included

The punk movement reached far beyond its music.

Rancid and The Distillers (from the US), Ikara Colt (from the UK) and Thee Michelle Gun Elephant and Guitar Wolf (from Japan) because they're great bands playing great punk rock right now.

So if your favourite punk song isn't here, I'm sorry. Actually no, I'm not.

If you don't like it, go write your own damn book.

"We're not going to go quietly to our deaths into some retirement home, eating Prozac. This is what they're planning for us, unless we do something about it. To always be a punk rocker is something everyone can do. And I mean that by attitude. ATTITUDE!"

Joe Strummer RIP

"Take no heroes/ Only inspiration"

The Redskins, "Take No Heroes"

The Adverts
One Chord Wonders

This was The Adverts' debut single on Stiff Records – home of such weird and wonderful mentalist mavericks and demented eccentrics as Wreckless Eric, Ian Dury, Lena Lovich and the young and hungry Elvis Costello.

The fanzine *Sniffin' Glue* (edited by Mark Perry who would later go on to form the band ATV) had made one of the definitive punk statements when it published that diagram of three guitar chords and the demand that readers now go and form their own band.

The Adverts went two better. "One Chord Wonders" sees the band setting themselves up as incompetent, fumbling, unlistenable clowns. Totally unable to play their instruments and hated by their audience. But not giving a damn – "I wonder how we'll answer when you say… Come back when you've learnt to play."

This was at least partly true. Live, The Adverts were a shambling mess. Deranged guitarist Howard Pickup stomped like a mad Frankenstein's monster through the hails of spit that greeted the band's every appearance. Achingly beautiful bassist Gaye Advert

(who, with her "panda" eye make-up, was an early icon for female punks) did a convincing impression of a leather-jacketed doe caught in the headlights of an oncoming juggernaut.

But what made The Adverts special was the amazing songwriting talents of singer Tim "TV" Smith. The guy was a genius. In the lyrics of "One Chord Wonders", Tim has the band looking up to discover that the audience has walked out in disgust.

"I had a band called Sleaze when I was at art college," remembers Tim. "They were a pretty poor prog-glam band that I started writing for as soon as I got out of school. So I'd already had the experience of going out there to present my work to the great British public – and discovering that they weren't interested in listening to some teenager banging on about his problems. I mean one time I actually did look up and the audience had gone!

"By the time I wrote the song I'd been to some Sex Pistols gigs. There was that feeling in the air that something was happening. Total joy and excitement. A band could get on stage and say – well we like what we're doing and we don't care what you think. That was the difference between going on stage in 1975 and going on stage in 1977. In 1977 you went on stage and said – well I like what I'm doing, fuck you! 'One Chord Wonders' was about what it was like being in a punk band. The sheer thrill of this music going on that wasn't under the grip of the music business. Just creativity and self-expression and just going out and doing it!

"It wasn't all totally aggressive guitar rock – which is what people think of when they think of punk today. There were loads of really eclectic groups about. All these strange little bands. Every band sounded totally different and they were coming up with these amazing lyrics. And they were all trying to say something. That's what punk rock means to me."

"One Chord Wonders" neatly summed up the punk spirit of just getting up and doing it. And to hell with the nitpickers, hippies, musos and "serious" rock critics. They didn't get it. It was their loss.

The original one chord wonders – The Adverts in 1977.

> ## "All you've got to do is learn a few chords, try and put a rhythm together, and if you've got something in your head then put it out. Who cares whether you can fucking play all the notes. I don't care. No one cares."

TV Smith, *New Wave News*, 1977

Gary Gilmore's Eyes

In 1977 I worked stacking shelves in a supermarket. The store played, over its Tannoy system, an endlessly looped tape of the current British Top 20. Not the originals, mind, but hideously saccharine "muzak" versions. Now this was fine as long as the records receiving this treatment were by the inoffensive likes of Abba or Boney M. But then The Adverts actually managed to have a hit record. With lyrics about mass murder, mutilation, organ transplantation and state execution. And, for a while, the usually boring supermarket job became a genuinely surreal experience.

One of the catchiest, wittiest and most gruesomely funny punk songs ever, "Gary Gilmore's Eyes" actually reached Number 18 in the British charts in 1977.

Gary Gilmore was a mentally ill American "spree killer" who became the first person to be executed when, in 1976, the US Supreme Court reinstated the death penalty. His story was famously told in Norman Mailer's book *The Executioner's Song*, which is widely regarded as a non-fictional literary classic.

But I'll take The Adverts' version any day, if only for the fact that it is absolutely hilarious.

The song recounts the paranoia and explosive rage of a poor chap who wakes up in hospital to discover that he's had Gilmore's eyes transplanted into his own gaping sockets. And it ends with the jaw-droppingly insensitive lyrical couplet: "Gary don't need his eyes to see/ Gary and his eyes have parted company."

"I didn't know much about Gary Gilmore, he was just in the news," admits Tim. "What I wanted to write was this little gothic horror story where Gilmore's retina gets transplanted into somebody else and the guy who gets it reads the newspaper and realizes it could be him. I mean transplant was meant to be secret, but I read about it in a newspaper that I picked out a rubbish bin in London.

"I was just writing about whatever I wanted to write about. That's one of the great things about a movement before the business gets its claws in – there's nobody telling you what to do. That's why punk was so diverse. I think 'Gary Gilmore's Eyes' was a novelty punk single. It was a joke horror song. But it did have a serious point. There was a Hammer Horror film called *The Hands Of Orlock* about a bloke who gets a murderer's hands transplanted onto his own wrists – so it was partly like that. But it was also making this existentialist point about how you perceive the world, how much is that to do with your actual physical body?

"In 1975 a band like Yes would have got a whole concept album out of that. And that's exactly the difference between prog rock and punk rock. We could just bung it on a three-minute joke single and we didn't have to flog it to death. At the time people said it was shocking and controversial. Was it bollocks! That was like going to see a Hammer film and saying that vampires and mummies were controversial.

"The lines about Gary and his eyes parting company came to me after the rest of the song. I was walking down the road, going to the shops and that just blasted into my head and I just fell about laughing in the middle of the street. I thought – that's got to go in! I don't care how sick it is, it's got to go in!"

And the weird thing is, I don't think anybody else in the supermarket ever noticed a thing.

ONE CHORD WONDERS / QUICKSTEP
SINGLE. STIFF RECORDS.
MAY 1977

GARY GILMORE'S EYES / BORED TEENAGERS
SINGLE. ANCHOR RECORDS.
SEPTEMBER 1977

"A leather-jacketed doe caught in the headlights of an oncoming juggernaut" – Gaye Advert.

Alternative TV
Love Lies Limp

The 1970s were known as the time of "the permissive society". The graphically illustrated book *The Joy Of Sex* was a bestseller, and sexual matters that would have been considered taboo for previous generations were increasingly being discussed openly in the mass media.

Western society seemed to be at last throwing off the smothering blanket of Victorian repression, and all was sweetness and light. Sex was hip and happening.

And so, of course, the punks declared themselves to be firmly against it.

Sexual liberation was too closely associated with the hippies of the 1960s. And anything the hippies were for, the punks were automatically against.

"Sex," said the Sex Pistols' Johnny Rotten, "is three minutes of squelching noises." The Buzzcocks' "Orgasm Addict" and Richard Hell's "Love Comes In Spurts" further articulated the anti-erotic punk consensus.

But none did it as dismally or with as much disgust as former bank clerk and fanzine editor Mark Perry. Originally released as a flexi-disc on the cover of *Sniffin' Glue* #12, "Love Lies Limp", with its "lazy cod-skank" take on reggae, also signalled Perry's determination to steer ATV away from what he saw as the homogenization of punk into just another form of rock music.

Angelic Upstarts
The Murder Of Liddle Towers

Britain is notorious for being the most snobbish, socially divided and class-conscious country in the world. So while punk was being trumpeted as a genuine working-class movement, this kind of overlooked the fact that some of its leading figures were actually a little bit, well, posh.

That couldn't be said of Mensi, the shaven-headed singer of the Upstarts who one cruel critic described as looking "like a bulldog licking piss off a nettle".

The Upstarts came from the economically depressed north-eastern English town of South Shields. They first came to national attention with a stunning live show in which the band, dressed in police uniforms, kicked a pig's head around the stage while blasting their way through a set of brutal yet melodic punk songs, many of which were about how much they hated the cops.

This was the subject of their first single, released on the DIY ("do-it-yourself") label in 1978. It starts with Mensi gently and eerily whispering "Who killed Liddle?/ Did you kill Liddle?" before erupting into an almost animal scream of rage, pain and frustration – "Police killed Liddle Towers!" Liddle was a local man who died, under somewhat controversial circumstances, in police custody.

"We used to sing the chorus at the cop in town on Friday nights, taking the piss out of the law," remembers Mensi. "We thought it was great so I put words to it and made a song up."

"Like a bulldog licking piss off a nettle" – Mensi and the Angelic Upstarts (plus female friend).

LOVE LIES LIMP
FREE FLEXI-DISC WITH
SNIFFIN' GLUE FANZINE #12.
1977

LIFE / LOVE LIES LIMP
SINGLE. DEPTFORD FUN CITY.
1978

THE MURDER OF LIDDLE
TOWERS / POLICE OPPRESSION
SINGLE. DIY. 1978

THE MURDER OF LIDDLE
TOWERS / POLICE OPPRESSION
SINGLE. SMALL WONDER.
MAY 1978

Bad Brains

Pay To Cum

Bad Brains have been described as "the greatest Rasta hardcore act ever". They were also, however, possibly the only Rasta hardcore band ever. For many of the London punk bands, the crossover between punk and reggae seemed obvious. Both were rebel music. Both made the authorities nervous. The Clash in particular were huge fans of dub reggae (and would later visit Jamaica). And many other punk bands attempted to introduce a reggae beat to their set (a tendency that would later result in the vile "new wave" abomination known as The Police).

1977, Washington DC. A guy known to his friends as HR is singer in a local all-black jazz/funk band. "We wanted to be part of something new and different and real," explains HR. "We was continually seeking. And then I saw the Sex Pistols album, and I said, 'BOOM! This is it!'"

They changed the band's name and started to play punk. They heard The Clash's version of the reggae classic "Police And Thieves". This led them to check out a Bob Marley concert – and become Rastafarians.

Moving to New York in 1979, the Brains released "Pay To Cum" on their own label. It is generally regarded as the first-ever record released by an American hardcore band.

Yet another punk sneer at the commercialization of sex, "Pay To Cum" was not only the fastest record anyone at the time had heard, it was also brilliant punk music being played by black guys. Which, to say the least, was pretty rare in the US music scene of the late 1970s.

The impact Bad Brains had on US hardcore punk (and subsequent attempts at multicultural crossover music, like rap-metal) has been absolutely enormous. But for many "Pay To Cum" remains their finest moment.

**BAD BRAINS
ALBUM. ROIR. 2001**

Bad Brains – the best Rasta hardcore band ever.

In the 1990s the punk phenomenon known as Riot Grrl exploded out of nowhere. Or so it seemed. It combined two ridiculously unfashionable philosophies – DIY punk and militant feminism.

Bikini Kill are seen by many to be the founders of Riot Grrl. The fact that they didn't possess a single penis among them was relevant only in that it chimed with their message of grrls-doing-it-for-themselves empowerment. But it also tended to obscure the fact that they were a fucking great punk band. And "Rebel Girl" is a great punk song – "When she talks I hear the revolution…In her kiss, I taste the revolution."

Karl Marx once wrote that "the purpose of philosophy is not to explain the world but to change it".

The anti-nazi playwright Bertol Brecht wrote: "Art is not a mirror. Art is a hammer."

Both those German dudes were proto-punk rockers.

Bikini Kill might not have changed the world, but they did inspire tens of thousands of young women to go out and try to change it for themselves. And that's what makes them a punk band.

Bikini Kill
Rebel Girl

Punk was meant to be above racism and sexism, but only an idiot would fail to notice that the overwhelming majority of its musicians, artists, fanzine writers and poets were white males. That said, women in bands before punk were as rare as hen's teeth. And all-women bands were even rarer.

THE CD VERSION OF THE FIRST TWO RECORDS ALBUM. KILL ALL ROCK STARS. 1996

Black Flag
Nervous Breakdown

When Black Flag delivered their debut album in 1981, MCA Records refused to release it, claiming that it was "immoral" and lacked "redeeming social value".

For a lot of the original London and New York punks, by 1979 the scene was already dead. How wrong they were. In Britain a bunch of black-clad extreme-vegan fanatics called Crass kick-started the whole anarcho-punk scene, while at the same time a new generation of working-class bands influenced by Sham 69 and the Angelic Upstarts coalesced around the banner of Oi!

But it was in America that punk was to have its real rebirth. Hardcore was about taking punk back to its roots. No frills, no fripperies and no compromise.

New York might rightly claim to be the US city that gave birth to American punk, but southern California was where it flourished and grew.

As rock writer Barney Hoskyns put it, hardcore was "younger, faster, angrier, full of the pent-up rage of dysfunctional Orange County adolescents who'd had enough of living in a bland Republican paradise".

And the Tyrannosaurus Rex of the hardcore scene were Black Flag. The LA-based band took punk's dalliance with musical and lyrical brutality to new extremes. One of their early concert flyers featured a police officer with a revolver in his mouth and the caption: "Make me come, faggot!" One of their early slogans was "What the fuck, fuck shit up!" Many gigs ended in full-scale battles between the band, their fans and the police. Perhaps more than any other band, Black Flag were the embodiment of punk as the music of confrontation.

And "Nervous Breakdown" is a classic example of how determined the US hardcore bands were to distance themselves from the cleaned-up and prettified "new wave" bands that were then just starting to tailcoat punk into the US charts.

I mean, check out this for in-your-face (and down-your-fucking-throat) lyrics: "I don't care what ya fuckin' do/ I don't care what ya fuckin' say/ I'm so sick of everything/ I just wanna die."

Henry Rollins raged as lead singer with Black Flag for ten years.

And all this, of course, was long before crazed and furious muscle-punk Henry Rollins joined the band.

NERVOUS BREAKDOWN
EP. SST. 1978

Blondie

Rip Her To Shreds

New Yorkers Blondie would, of course, go on to become a massively successful pop band. But they always were a pop band. There was nothing terribly contradictory about this. For the early punks, boring, old, hairy, self-indulgent and self-important rock music was the enemy, not pop.

Manager Malcolm McLaren always said that he saw the Sex Pistols as "the new Bay City Rollers" (the biggest "manufactured" boy band of the late 1970s). And The Ramones had similar ambitions.

Blondie have pop kudos by the bucketload. Not only did they have the ability to write incredibly catchy songs but they were also possessed, in the shape of the beautiful Debbie Harry, of a singer who was destined to become punk's first (and perhaps only) mainstream sex symbol. And they also had style – the boys in sharp mod suits and ties, Debbie looking like an infinitely more worldly wise version of the young Marilyn Monroe.

In fact, Blondie looked nothing like a stereotypical punk band. Which, of course, made them one hell of a lot punkier than the bands that did.

And "Rip Her To Shreds" – in which Harry confesses her desire to use a knife on a sexual rival – is most definitely a punk song.

I mean, "all she needs is an old knife scar". That's just not nice, is it?

Denis

"Denis", on the other hand, is perfect bubblegum pop. Whereas the moronic genius of The Ramones was always just a little too brutal for the wider American public to appreciate, Blondie were always destined for pop stardom. And this, more than any other song, is the single that blasted them into the mainstream. "Denis" was a slick cover of a 1963 doo-wop hit by Randy And The Rainbows. It was a worldwide hit. For Blondie, the incestuous, violent and exciting world of the New York punk scene was soon to be nothing but a memory.

Left: "Blondie are a band."

Right: "Oh yeah?" The stunningly beautiful Debbie Harry.

Hanging On The Telephone

Hardly surprisingly for a band consisting of a bunch of average-looking chaps and one achingly beautiful blonde woman, most people thought that Debbie Harry was Blondie. The band took to handing out "Blondie is a band" badges, but that was just pissing in the wind.

"Hanging On The Telephone" is probably Blondie's finest hour. It combines the aggression of their punk roots with the knack for a slick pop hook that was both the band's greatest blessing and their biggest curse.

They were also to have hits with, among others, the "alternative disco" "Heart Of Glass" and the sublime "Tide Is High". But American punk, meanwhile, had moved on (or moved backwards, depending on your point of view). By the early '80s the US was experiencing the primitive, aggressive and brutally fast joys of the hardcore punk explosion. But by that time Blondie existed in another universe entirely.

BLONDIE
ALBUM. PRIVATE STOCK. 1976
(RE-ISSUED BY CHRYSALIS
1979)

PLASTIC LETTERS
ALBUM. CHRYSALIS. 1978

PARALLEL LINES
ALBUM. CHRYSALIS. 1978

Boomtown Rats
I Don't Like Mondays

OK, I admit it. The Boomtown Rats were fakes. They were plastic punks. They were Johnny-come-lately bandwagon jumpers. But you know what? I don't give a damn.

Fronted by ex-music journalist Bob Geldoff (who would achieve international fame in the 1980s as the organizer of the Live Aid/Band Aid charity events), the Rats had a series of wacky charts hits in the UK in the late 1970s and early '80s.

"I Don't Like Mondays" tells the tale, in a chillingly matter-of-fact way, of pretty 16-year-old Californian high-school student Brenda Spencer. One Monday morning in January 1979, Brenda grabbed her father's gun and opened fire on her school from across the street. Eight pupils were injured and two people died, including the school's principal.

When asked why she'd done it, Brenda replied: "I just started shooting, that's it. I just did it for the fun of it. I just don't like Mondays. I just did it because it's a way to cheer the day up. Nobody likes Mondays."

The song was a hit on both sides of the Atlantic, despite being banned by many radio stations in the US.

And if that isn't punk, I don't know what is.

I DON'T LIKE MONDAYS /
IT'S ALL THE RAGE
SINGLE. ENSIGN. 1979

The Boomtown Rats trying very, very hard to look punk.

The Buzzcocks

What Do I Get

"I just want a lover like any other/ What do I get?"

One of the "rules" of punk was that you didn't sing about romantic love. This is neatly illustrated in the origin of The Clash song "I'm So Bored With The USA". Guitarist Mick Jones had written a song about an ex-girlfriend and given it the title "I'm So Bored With You".

Clash singer Joe Strummer misheard the title. "That's brilliant!" said Strummer, thinking Mick had written a stinging attack on American cultural imperialism.

"No, no – it's about my girlfriend!" explained Mick.

"Not any more!" said Joe.

For the sneering, cynical, political punks, "lurrve" was only mentioned if it could be mocked or subverted. It was one of pop's biggest clichés – a horse that had been flogged ceaselessly since the 1950s. Punk was about breaking the mould, about burning the house down. It was a Year Zero. And love was out of bounds.

The Buzzcocks broke the rule.

After seeing the Sex Pistols in 1976, a bunch of lads from the northern English city of Manchester decided to form their own band. In this they were far from unique, but the music they came up with was exceptional.

Scraping together £100, they made the now legendary (and much sought after) *Spiral Scratch* EP. It was only the third British punk record ever released, and it was the first to embody the DIY ethic (alongside the Desperate Bicycles, The Buzzcocks more or less invented the independent punk scene). And it was brilliant.

Singer Howard Devoto (a balding, creepy-voiced uber-nerd who looked as if he'd be more at home in a horror comic than fronting a band) left soon after to go back to college (Devoto would later found the band Magazine). And the wonky-faced (and wonky-voiced) Pete Shelley took over on vocals.

The band soon signed to a major label but the fantastic songs kept on coming.

"What Do I Get?" is a classic example of The Buzzcocks' ability to write a brilliantly catchy, buzzsaw-guitared, pop-punk whine about what love is actually like for "the rest of us". For the nerds, geeks and losers. For the ugly and the inadequate. For the clumsy and frustrated. It turned the macho bluster of heavy metal on its empty head. It totally subverted pop's obsession with love. It asked the question: if love is so great, why aren't I getting any?

And in doing so said more about the reality of the average teenage male's so-called sex life than The Beatles and their ilk had ever done.

Ever Fallen In Love With Someone (You Shouldn't Have)

"You disturb my natural emotions/ You make me feel like dirt"

Punk intellectual Kevin Mekon once stated that the perfect record would "sound like a cross between Abba and the Sex Pistols". Many have tried to achieve that demented blend – indeed "pop punk" has now become an almost meaningless cliché.

But The Buzzcocks pulled it off – and they did it brilliantly. Pop philosopher David Quantick has argued that "the difference between pop and rock is this: pop tells you something you already know and says – isn't that amazing? While rock tells you something you already know and says – Gosh, aren't I clever?"

By that definition, The Buzzcocks were definitely a pop band. "Ever Fallen In Love With Someone (You Shouldn't Have)" asked a question that every single audience member could only answer in the affirmative.

(I mean, come on, be honest, you've fallen in love with someone you shouldn't have, haven't you?)

But it did so on your terms. From your perspective. It was the plaintive whine of the sexually frustrated and romantically devastated everyman underdog. Yes it was pop. Damn catchy pop (for all its super-punky speed and aggression). But lyrically it took pop into places it had never been before – and didn't really want to visit.

Nearly all pop songs are about love, and most make one of two statements: boo-hoo, my boy/girlfriend's left me; or whoopee-do, isn't love great? The Buzzcocks took pop's promise of love and kicked it around the recording studio, asking: why doesn't this work the way you promised it would?

Instead of ignoring pop's biggest cliché, The Buzzcocks met it head on and subverted it. One of the ways it did this was through Pete Shelley's voice. The working-class Manchester accent sounds, to most ears, slightly camp. This, added to Shelley's distinctly unmacho demeanour, meant that you never really knew if he was singing about a boy or a girl or both.

Compared to the macho likes of their contemporaries – the Pistols, Clash and Damned – The Buzzcocks were as camp as a row of tents. (In 1981, Shelley's solo single "Homosapien" was banned by the BBC for "explicit references to gay sex", specifically the lyric "homo superior/ in my interior".)

Jon Savage, music journalist and author of the brilliant, definitive Sex Pistols biography *England's Dreaming*, has written extensively about punk's "secret" gay roots. They're not hard to find (if you're willing to look). Indeed, the word punk itself has its origins in the pre-gay-liberation homosexual underworld.

This is not to say that punk is gay, or even that most people who've got involved in punk over the decades are aware of its gay connections, but punk is – or should be – about subversion. About confusion. About fucking with the heads of Mr and Mrs Straight. And the effete savagery of The Buzzcocks most definitely did that.

Pete Shelley – bisexual punk genius.

Orgasm Addict

"You get in a heat, you get in a sulk/ but you still keep a beating your meat to pulp"

The 1970s were seen by many as a period of sexual liberation and adventure. The contraceptive pill had been invented and HIV/AIDS were as yet unheard of. As a result, sex became commercialized as never before in human history.

Punk regarded all this with suspicion and cynicism. Many of the male punks dressed like New York male prostitutes, while the girls – with their plastic garbage bag dresses, stockings and hideously exaggerated make-up – looked like caricatures of S&M whores.

The Buzzcocks' "Orgasm Addict" articulated this cynical critique of "free love" brilliantly. Basically, it's about wanking. Jerking off. Spanking the monkey. And – surprise, surprise – it didn't receive a great deal of daytime radio plays.

Anticipating that the single would be banned, The Buzzcocks issued a statement: " 'Orgasm Addict' is an anti-sex song emphasizing the dehumanizing of personal relationships. The flip side, 'Whatever Happened To', describes both the love object of a supermarket society and the process that transforms nostalgia and romance into yet more consumer goods."

This was heavy stuff, but it made little difference. The song had "orgasm" in the title and "fuck" in the lyrics. It was banned.

Delivered in Shelley's trademark "fey whine" and featuring a tragi-comic parody of the male orgasm, "Addict" is simultaneously one of the funniest and most depressing punk songs ever. And also one of the most honest. Given that most of The Buzzcocks' audience were adolescent males, this was about their real, actual sex lives. For most of them, most of the time, self-gratification was the only action they were getting.

In *England's Dreaming*, author Jon Savage writes: " 'Orgasm Addict' finally admits the laughter that is too often banned from sex. With Devoto's packed, polymorphous lyrics set off perfectly by Shelley's casual swearing, heavy breathing and simulated orgasms. The tension between Shelley's ludicrous camp squeals and the group thundering behind him is terrific. The images flash past you like a scene from a humorous porno loop, there is a brief guitar stutter, Shelley shouts out the title phrase, and it's all over – in one minute 59 seconds."

There have, of course, been other records about the "sin of onanism", but nearly all of them have taken an indirect and ambiguous approach. But there's no mistaking what "Orgasm Addict" is about. It was to remain the most honest record ever made about teenage male sexuality until the release of Ivor Biggun's comedy-punk single "The Wanker's Song". But that's another, altogether less edifying, story.

SPIRAL SCRATCH
EP. NEW HORMONES.
JANUARY 1977 (RE-ISSUED
1979)

SINGLES GOING STEADY
COMPILATION ALBUM.
IRS.1979

"Heavy breathing and simulated orgasms" – The Buzzcocks.

Circle Jerks
World Up My Ass

A "circle jerk" is a group activity (popular in the military and in private schools) that involves a group of males masturbating onto a cookie, the idea being that the chap who comes last then has to eat the cookie.

The Circle Jerks were the band formed by singer Keith Morris when he left Black Flag. The beer-fuelled Morris described his role in Black Flag as "the Tasmanian devil, the court jester; I was the dog on the chain who was let out of the cage".

But The Circle Jerks, amazingly, were even faster, more brutal, much dumber and infinitely less subtle than Black Flag – and that took some doing.

Their first album, *Group Sex* (featuring "World Up My Ass"), smashed its way through 14 demented songs in just 16 minutes. It was about as subtle as a fist in the face – and just about as welcome for most rock critics. US hardcore bands like the Circle Jerks split the US "alternative" record-buying public right down the middle. You either revelled in the brutality, nihilism, violence and rage of hardcore or it utterly repelled you.

Many of the "original" punk bands had, in the meantime, mellowed and matured, and the major record companies were foisting a sanitized version of punk (known as "new wave") on an ignorant public.

The Circle Jerks just didn't wanna to know. They were taking punk back to basics – and beyond. And that's why "World Up My Ass" is in this book and The Knack's "My Sherona" isn't.

> "Take a bite then spit it out/ Take their rules – rip 'em up"

**GROUP SEX
ALBUM. FRONTIER. 1981**

The Clash

White Riot

After the Sex Pistols, The Clash were the most influential punk band ever.

By 1976 rock music had become a bloated self-parody – an ageing generation of ex-hippie millionaire superstars living a luxury lifestyle, totally out of touch with the kids who bought their records.

In Britain and America the kids were listening to somebody else's music, dressing up in somebody else's clothes, taking somebody else's drugs and feverishly puffing on the ditched roach of the previous generation's culture. Something had to change – and it did. Two bands – The Clash and the Sex Pistols – kick-started a musical revolution. 1976 was the year of punk.

The snarling, spitting Sex Pistols were never going to last. They were too explosive, too destructive, too fuelled by self-loathing and hatred.

The Clash were different. They were out to change not just the haircuts, clothes and musical tastes of a generation, but they were also out to change the world. They were truly radical. Where the Sex Pistols offered nihilism, The Clash offered revolution.

Before starting The Clash, diplomat's son Joe Strummer had been singing with the pub rock band The 101ers. Guitarist Mick Jones and bassist Paul Simenon were in a band called London SS. None of them was a great musician (Paul had learned to play from scratch in a matter of weeks), but in 1976 that suddenly no longer mattered. The basic tenet of punk was that anybody could form a rock band. And thousands of kids all over the the US and the UK

They fought the record industry and the record industry won. The Clash in full "rebel" mode.

> "All the power's in the hands of people rich enough to buy it/ While we walk the streets too chicken to even try it"

(and later the world) did just that. But none of them did it better than The Clash.

Mick, Joe and Paul got together after seeing the Sex Pistols and being "totally blown away". Paul – an artist and a fan of "splatter" painter Jackson Pollock – came up with the name. Bernie Rhodes, their manager, was partly responsible for steering the band into a more political direction.

But what made The Clash special was the songs. Their first album – the self-titled *The Clash* – was the first great album of the punk era. It had a rough, rushed feel that was a million light years from the slick and polished product of the rock mainstream. Strummer's harsh, glottal-stopped lyrics were sometimes almost indecipherable. It was raw. It was angry. It was overtly political and sounded as if it had been made in a frenzy

The Clash (with drummer Topper Headon) on their infamous trip to Belfast.

of impatience. And it was exactly what an entire generation had been waiting for.

In the words of US journalist Tom Carson: "As a documentary of rock'n'roll teenagers battling first for good times and then for survival in a blasted urban landscape, The Clash's debut album...had an astonishing immediacy. You got the feeling that it was recorded virtually in the street, while the National Front marched and the threat of riots flickered all around...Perhaps more than any album ever made, The Clash dramatized rock'n'roll as a last, defiantly cheerful grab for life, something scrawled on the run on subway walls."

I remember the day I saw THAT sleeve. Three surly spiked neo-mods in harsh monochrome, framed by ripped olive-green. And on the back a photo of the previous year's riot at the Notting Hill Carnival, the song titles splattered below in Day-Glo orange typewriter capitals. That sleeve burns my brain. It was devastating. A napalm strike on the soul. And the sleeve was an accurate reflection of the music within. This music was primitive, clumsy even, but it was also wildly radical, incredibly intense and utterly addictive. The Clash adopted and adapted the trebly guitar, skittering drums and rumbling bass of the reggae music that they loved and married it to the attack-dog malevolence of punk. Every song had a message. Every line shoved two fingers up at authority. And every copy sold created a score of new, excited and radicalized fans. It was, in short, the perfect punk record.

It's the first record that I ever fell in love with.

It seethed with ideas. The staccato drums and reggae-style instrument drop-outs seemed revolutionary to ears trained on chart pop and the pompous excesses of "progressive rock".

The lyrics were a glottal stew, but it was obvious that all the right targets – boredom, unemployment, pacifism, corporatism, consumerism, the police – were being lined up and kicked to oblivion.

This record is ABOUT something. It's an extended musical tantrum. It's the sound of a mob storming a museum. Of something young and strong and fresh and

extremely pissed off bursting out of the bloated corpse of a co-opted youth culture – like the chest-buster from *Alien* on speed.

Punk, meantime, had come to the attention of the mainstream media. The tabloid press had a new folk devil to crucify. The kids had a new way to wind up teachers and parents. And – in the sullen, swaggering, spiky, angry and articulate Clash – they had a new template of what a band should be, of what a band could be.

The Clash weren't just a bunch of musicians. In fact some argued that they weren't technically skilled enough to be considered musicians at all. They were a gang, a bunch of dead cool-looking troublemakers. In every interview the band preached the punk gospel of empowerment. Think for yourself, take control of your own destiny, refuse the future that society has planned for you, question authority – and do it now.

In 1978 The Clash headlined the first big Anti-Nazi League concert in London's Victoria Park. In the UK the far-right National Front had been growing in popularity, scapegoating Britain's immigrant community even as the tensions between black kids and the police reached boiling point and as the UK started its long slide into mass unemployment. Up to this point most of the punk bands had been studiously apolitical, some of them even sporting swastikas as a shock tactic.

The Clash changed all that. They put themselves firmly behind the newly formed Rock Against Racism and a host of other radical causes. They made rock political for the first time since the 1960s – and their legacy lingers even today.

But The Clash, inevitably, were also fast becoming the very thing they set out to destroy. The ex-skinhead (Paul), the wannabe guitar hero (Mick) and the pub rocker (Joe) were sold to the masses as rock stars. Some of the time they revelled in their newfound status, and some of the time they rebelled against it. They were permanently at war with their record company and, increasingly, with each other.

When the end came in 1984 it was, inevitably, messy, but the legacy of The Clash lives on. They have inspired generations of radical rock bands – from Rage Against The Machine to System Of A Down, from the Manic Street Preachers to The Strokes.

Mick Jones and Joe Strummer (in gargoyle mode).

Tick off all The Clash's faults, list all their failures, broken promises and mistakes, and you're still left with the much greater reality of the band who redefined rock'n'roll as a music of protest, riot, rage and liberation.

Today, The Clash still matter and their influence is massive. They've left behind a template – the idea of the band as a gang, the band as an on-stage riot, as flawed gurus. The band as guerrillas, as preachers and propagandists, as revolutionaries, rabble rousers and rebel rockers. That template is still valid, and it continues to make all the other proffered alternatives look lame, weak, pasty-faced and pitiful by comparison.

And they've also left behind some brilliant songs.

"White Riot" (and I could have picked any of the tracks off the first Clash album) was widely misunderstood. The nazis of the National Front even tried to claim it as an anthem for their own sick and twisted racist agenda. They couldn't have been more wrong.

In August 1976, Paul, Joe and manager Bernie had attended west London's Notting Hill Carnival. The event had often been the scene of confrontations between black youths and the police, and this year was to be no different.

There were to be 60 arrests and over 450 injuries. During what can only be described as a riot, Paul slung a traffic cone at a police motorcyclist and then he and Strummer spent several hours bombarding the police line with whatever they could find to throw.

"It was brilliant!" remembered Paul. "The coppers were just standing there and they couldn't do a thing. We could throw bricks right at 'em. It was great!"

The riot was to prove a formative experience for The Clash, and a direct inspiration for one of their greatest songs. "We know the blacks've got their thing sewn up," said guitarist Mick Jones. "They've got their own culture but the young white kids don't have nothing. That's why so many of them are living in ignorance and they've gotta wise up…They used to blame everything on the Jews, now they're saying it about the blacks and the Asians. Everyone's a scapegoat, right?"

With its call for a riot "of my own", "White Riot" is a plea for white kids to become as militant and as angry as black kids. But, more than that, it asks them to direct their anger at the real enemy – the powers that be – rather than at racial minorities. "We're hoping to educate any kid who comes to listen to us," said Joe. "Just to keep 'em from joining the National Front when things get tough in a couple of years."

The punk scene in Britain had already had more than a few flirtations with fascism. The northern city of Leeds had even seen the formation of the "punk front", which featured several NF-supporting punk bands. And, in his book *Bovver*, ex-skinhead and ex-football hooligan Chris Brown reveals that, in many other British cities, the nazis were already targeting punks with their racist propaganda.

Far from being a fascist anthem, "White Riot" was in fact where punk developed an anti-racist social conscience.

In November 2002, Mick Jones appeared on stage with Joe Strummer for the last time. Joe introduced the song by saying to Mick: "This one's in A, you know it."

A month later Joe Strummer died of a heart attack.

Complete Control

"They said we'd be artistically free when we signed that bit of paper/ They meant let's make a lotsa money and worry about it later"

Unpromisingly, "Complete Control" is a song in which The Clash whine about their record company, CBS.

CBS had pressured the band into releasing "Remote Control" (a track off their first album) as a single. "Complete Control" was written in response. In retrospect it all seems a little sad and self-indulgent.

At the time, UK punk was bursting out of its cliquey London ghetto and reaching millions of provincial kids. Many of these kids were fired up by The Clash's talk of

"doing it for themselves". And were doing just that. They were forming their own bands, writing their own fanzines and starting up their own DIY record labels.

And here were The Clash, signed to a major label, bitching because they hadn't read the small print on their contract. The song had echoes of John Lennon's "The Ballad Of John And Yoko", in which the ex-Beatle moaned about press harassment. Aw diddums! Pity the poor rock stars!

But the fact remains that it's a fucking great song – one of the band's best. Even if the subject matter was self-indulgent, the spiteful, sarcastic anger of Joe Strummer's vocals still send a thrill down the spine.

In his book *The 500 Greatest Singles Since Punk And Disco*, Gary Mulholland writes: "Having applied for the job as punk's conscience and quickly found themselves drowning under the contradiction of being socialist rebels signed to a huge multinational, The Clash freaked at the humiliation...Joe is lost in his own fury, gabbling with incoherent anger while the guitars and backing vocals shower him in tears of frustration. Innocence lost. From now on, it was a fight to the inevitable death."

It seemed The Clash were at a stage where they were incapable of writing a shit song, even when the subject matter was less than edifying.

English Civil War

1978's *Give 'Em Enough Rope* – the second Clash album – came as something of a shock. Sandy Pearlman's slick production job was obviously aimed at the American market. You could hear the words! And it didn't sound as if it was recorded down the bottom of a well. Sharp, aggressive and much "rockier" than the first album, *Rope* also featured some of the best Clash material to date.

Musically, "English Civil War" is based on the old American Civil War song "When Johnny Comes Marching Home", but lyrically it represented The Clash's take on the nightmare dictatorship that was predicted in George Orwell's classic dystopian sci-fi novel, *1984*. "Your face was blue in the light of the screen as we watched the speech of an animal scream/ the new party army was marching right over our heads."

In 1978 the far-right National Front were still threatening to become a major electoral force in British politics. In 1979 the right-wing Conservative Party leader Margaret Thatcher came to power in Britain (a situation reflected in the US two years later with the election of Ronald Reagan as president). Thatcher – a long-standing and unashamed defender of the racist apartheid regime in South Africa – had made a speech in which she attacked racial minorities, claiming that "British values" were in danger of being "swamped by an alien culture".

For several years The Clash had been allied to Rock Against Racism and the Anti-Nazi League, but there were many that feared that fascism would come into power though the front door, rather than the back.

In retrospect this might seem naïve, but at the time the fear was very real. "English Civil War" proved that The Clash still had the ability to write songs that accurately reflected – and predicted – the political climate.

While "English Civil War" climbed into the UK Top 30, one-and-a-half million British public service workers went on strike. Uncollected garbage piled up in the street, right-wing tabloid newspapers screamed about

bodies being left unburied, the Labour government seemed paralyzed – and Mrs Thatcher was just around the corner.

The song attracted flak at the time from critics who regarded it as an hysterical over-reaction. Guitarist Mick Jones replied: "In 1928, Adolf Hitler got 2.8% of the vote. By 1939, there was no one voting for anybody else."

(White Man) In Hammersmith Palais

"(White Man) In Hammersmith Palais" is probably The Clash's finest moment. In fact, I'd rate it as one of the top ten rock/pop singles of all time, which is odd because "WMIHP" is based around two themes – both parochial, and both very much of their time.

The first is Joe Strummer's memory of a reggae concert he'd recently been to. All is not sweetness and light. Robberies are taking place and Strummer admits to feeling more than a little uncomfortable as one of only a few white faces among a crowd of suspicious and hostile black ones. The call for white kids to get out there and chuck bricks at the police in solidarity with their oppressed black brethren (as articulated in "White Riot") is absent. Here, Joe is no fire-breathing rabble rouser. He's a scared little white guy reduced to pleading that he's "just looking for fun".

Had that been all, "WMIHP" would still have been a remarkably honest song, especially from someone who had associated himself so closely with the politics of anti-racism, but Strummer goes further. He draws a parallel between the concert and the state of UK punk. The Sex Pistols had just split, The Clash were engaged in a slanging match with The Jam – and punk's early promise of changing not just the music business but the whole damn world was looking increasingly empty.

And if that had been the full of extent of Strummer's lyrical ambition, that too would have been truly remarkable. But no, he goes even further. He paints

the state of punk as a metaphor for the disintegration of society in general. And then he hits us with the truly shocking lines: "All over people changing their votes along with their overcoats/ If Adolf Hitler flew in today, they'd send a limousine anyway."

Musically, "WMIHP" is no less impressive than its lyrics. It's The Clash's most confident and assured foray into the reggae music they loved so much. The cover version of Junior Marvin's reggae classic "Police And Thieves" on their first album was remarkable more for its inclusion than for the band's ability to reproduce anything that sounded at all like authentic reggae. But while "WMIHP" doesn't sound like it was recorded in Trenchtown, Jamaica, nor does it sound at all awkward or clumsy. It is the perfect fusion of reggae and punk.

Listening back to the musical and lyrical leaps of imagination on "WMIHP" today, it seems remarkable that it was made by a band who, only a few years earlier, had been blasting out primitive, hollering blasts of semi-articulate rage that were only thinly disguised as songs.

THE CLASH
ALBUM. CBS. 1978

GIVE 'EM ENOUGH ROPE
ALBUM. CBS. 1978

LONDON CALLING
ALBUM. CBS. 1979

COMPLETE CONTROL
SINGLE. CBS. 1977

WHITE MAN IN
HAMMERSMITH PALAIS
SINGLE. CBS. 1978

Joe Strummer and the incredibly handsome Paul Simmenon.

The Cramps

Garbageman

The Cramps looked like a bourbon-soaked, sulphate-addled and only slightly more photogenic Addams Family. They sounded like a primitive swamp-rockabilly version of Siouxsie And The Banshees – except much, much funnier.

They've even been described as a "surf" band, which would be true if surf music had originated in the Louisiana bayou rather than on the beaches of southern California (now there's an image).

Had they come along a few years later, they would probably have been dismissed as "psychobilly", but at the time The Cramps were rightly regarded as one of punk's weirdest offshoots.

"Garbageman" was the flip side to a cover of Peggy Lee's classic diva-fatale anthem "Fever". It was also the track that got played the most in all the truly hip clubs and on all the grooviest radio stations.

It perhaps represents The Cramps most successful attempt to distil their unique schlock-horror trash-aesthetic and to write the soundtrack to a peculiarly American voodoo-gothic (not a million miles from that achieved by comic writer Alan Moore during his now legendary stint on DC's *Swamp Thing*).

Swampy guitars drone over insane drumming as singer Lux Interior delivers what appears to be total gibberish (in the voice, of course, of a mad demon-possessed southern Baptist preacher): "You ain't no punk, you punk. You wanna talk about the real junk? If I ever slip, I'll be banned 'cause I'm your Garbageman… Now do you understand? Do you understand?"

Er, well, no, not really. "Garbageman" was about the sterility of the mainstream vision – dull, generic rock bands citing other equally dull and equally generic rock bands as "influences". And it mocked the sad fact that nobody was bothering to go back and check out the real, dirty, obscure and dangerous stuff – "the real junk".

GARBAGEMAN / FEVER
SINGLE. ILLEGAL. 1980 (UK)

GARBAGEMAN / DRUG TRAIN
SINGLE. IRS. 1980 (US)

The Cramps' Lux Interior auditions for the Royal Ballet.

Crass

Do They Owe Us A Living (Well?...Do They?)

Ah, Crass! Many punk bands have been accused of making an unlistenable row, but in the case of Crass this was literally true. They were awful! One critic described them as sounding like "two lathes buggering each other on an elevator in an aircraft hangar". But they are also one of the most influential rock bands ever.

Crass arrived on the scene proclaiming "punk is dead", and promptly set about totally revitalizing the genre. "I think that we've been largely responsible for restating a set of ideas which have roots way back through history," says band member Peter Wright. "These are quite simply – sod all authority. I as an individual have something worthwhile about me."

When the Sex Pistols split and The Clash started releasing three-disc concept albums and the UK punk dream was generally regarded as having died on its tired, safety-pinned ass, left behind was an audience radicalized by the fight against the fascists, by disillusionment with the Labour Party, by the left-wing rhetoric of The Clash and by a literal interpretation of the Pistols' "anarchy". The demise of UK punk Mark I left a vacuum that would be filled by bands preaching spiky-haired peace and love. In the UK at least, the "real" anarchists would inherit the punk earth.

Crass were a mixture of newly cropped 1960s hippie-libertarians, art-college graduates and bitterly disillusioned gut-reaction Clash fans. They were fuelled and inspired by an exciting mish-mash of Kerouac, *Last Exit To Brooklyn*, Kropotkin, Situationism and, perhaps above all else, the example of Italian Autonomism. They professed a belief in the literal truth of the idealistic anti-authoritarian manifestos that had dribbled from the curled lips of the now discredited first wave of London art-school punks.

At the peak of their popularity, Crass were shifting 100,000 copies of every single record they released. Considering their total refusal to have anything to do with the mass media, their popularity was staggering. They pulled off some remarkable publicity coups, particularly over the Falklands War and the wedding of Prince Charles and Lady Diana. Apoplectic conservative politicians went so far as to demand police action to shut them up. Crass's constituency was a broad swathe of usually unemployed, alienated and disenfranchized youth who would brook no compromise with the system. At all.

Crass shows were stunning visual experiences. Against a backdrop of Japanese "peace" banners and banks of static-spewing televisions, Crass ran around the stage like demented cyberpunk Vietcong. They screamed, spat and roared their passionate hatred of all forms of authority. Crass were pissed off – about everything! And boy did they let you know.

Crass were for peace and anarchy. They were against nuclear weapons (any weapons, actually, but nukes in particular), capitalism, patriarchy, sexism, racism, state communism, the police, the government (all governments) and eating meat. And they almost single-handedly founded the genre of anarcho-punk.

Anarcho-punks wore black. And they didn't wear leather or eat meat or drink milk (and tended to be smugly hostile to those who did). Anarcho-punk fanzines would run lists of "names" in the scene who had allegedly been seen eating "murdered" animals, hitting a heckler or (horror of horrors) putting milk in their tea.

The passion and commitment of the kids who followed Crass were amazing. They made the original punks look like part-time dabblers. These kids preached the gospel of Crass 24/7. They became known as "Crasstafarians" – a pun on "Rastafarians" that acutely underscored their almost religious fervour. Hardly surprisingly, the rest of society generally regarded anarcho-punks as a thoroughgoing pain in the ass.

Soon there were hundreds of bands that sounded exactly like Crass. By the mid-'80s, Crass were like the false prophet in *The Life Of Brian*.

"Piss off!" they'd roar at the hordes of dress-a-like, sound-a-like anarcho-clones.

"And how shall we piss off?" roared back the sheep...

"You'd end up with 40 bands doing songs about cruise missiles, all dressed in black," moaned Crass member Steve Ignorant. "I got to the stage where I

thought – if I hear one more bastard song about Cruise bastard missiles!"

Crass put out their DIY records with copious, brilliantly designed booklets containing loads of useful information about smashing the system and some truly brilliant political photomontages. A cartoon of the time shows a mohawked punk walking into a record shop and buying a Crass album. He promptly takes the record out, sticks it in the garbage can and walks off, eagerly reading the booklet.

So why are they in this book then? Because Crass were vital for punk's survival. Because they guaranteed the continuation of punk as a platform for protest (rather than just another form of rock music) for decades to come. And because "DTOUAL" is one of the definitive punk statements.

The basic message of "DTOUAL" is summed up in the lines: "Owe us a living? OF COURSE THEY FUCKING DO!" This is a statement that flies in the face of the protestant work ethic, the American dream and every other philosophy that the respectable middle classes cling to in order that they might remain sane in their unceasing holy struggle against the forces of darkness and disorder. And it is, therefore, thoroughly punk rock.

Crass – radical politics, discordant music, terrible haircuts.

thousands and – through their political activism as much as their music – sowed the seeds of today's worldwide anti-globalization and anti-capitalist movements.

"We're inseparable from the entire youth movement," says Rimbaud. "What we contributed was so broad, and so powerful, so invasive, that I think it's in everything. I certainly think without Crass, punk would have had no effect at all.

"It was us that introduced a meaningful overview into what was then called punk."

And today, when the world's fat cats, bankers, planet rapers and sold-out politicians peer out past the police barriers at the mass of anarchy flag-waving protesters beyond and mutter, "That lot think the world owes them a living…" the mob replies "OF COURSE YOU FUCKING DO!"

And it doesn't get more punk than that.

THE FEEDING OF
THE FIVE THOUSAND
ALBUM. CRASS RECORDS.
1978

STATIONS OF THE CRASS
ALBUM. CRASS RECORDS.
1979

"We weren't a band for musical or lyrical reasons," admits Crass's Penny Rimbaud. "We were a band for political reasons…We weren't a band. We never were a band. I don't think we even saw ourselves as a band…We certainly didn't belong in the sort of pantomime of rock'n'roll, and probably even less in the pantomime of what became known as punk. It wasn't our interest. I mean, we weren't interested in making records. We were interested in making statements."

Crass were more than just a band, in the same way that punk was more than just music. In their brief but incredibly influential career, they touched the lives of

Culturcide

They Aren't The World

Long before sampling became commonplace (and way, way before all the fuss about Napster), Houston-based punk pranksters Culturcide had the brilliant idea of just singing over other people's records and then putting the results out as their own work. This, of course, drove the record industry insane with anger and established Culturcide as underground punk legends.

Released in 1986, *Tacky Souvenirs Of Pre-Revolutionary America* was, in the words of one critic, "a blatantly illegal work of manic-dub genius". Culturcide took a bunch of pop hits, changed the titles, sang their own sardonic and subversive lyrics over the top, added some mental noises – and then stood back to await the inevitable shit storm with glee.

Among the sacred pop-cows that received this hilarious and brutal treatment were Paul McCartney, Michael Jackson and Bruce Springsteen, but the stand-out track was an amazing – almost sacrilegious – debunking of the Live Aid/Band Aid single "We Are The World".

"We Are The World" was a megastar-studded charity record released to raise funds to help people starving in Africa. It was good people doing a good thing in a good cause, and as such it was beyond criticism. But nobody told Culturcide this.

On "They Aren't The World" (while the likes of Lionel Richie, Stevie Wonder, Paul Simon and Billy Joel can be heard bleating piously in the background), Culturcide sing: "There comes a time when rock stars beg for cash…There are people dying/ whooaah and they just noticed…"

"They're Not The World" was subversive on many levels. As it rightly pointed out, there was something profoundly obscene about rich western pop stars trying to raise money to feed people in a world that actually creates a surplus of food, but what really upset the music industry was the flagrant and outrageous breach of its sacred copyright laws.

The lawyers descended. Culturcide were driven out of existence, but *Tacky Souvenirs* is now a collector's item – and it still contains lessons for any punk rocker out there who really (I mean really) wants to piss off the music industry.

TACKY SOUVENIRS OF PRE-REVOLUTIONARY AMERICA ALBUM. GREY MATTER. 1987

The Damned

New Rose

The Damned's Captain Sensible and Dave Vanian.

"The Damned, much as I love them, were just hell-for-leather destruction merchants," sighs (now older and wiser) Damned bassist Captain Sensible.

If The Clash were punk's Beatles and the Sex Pistols were its Rolling Stones (and people really were writing rubbish like this at the time), The Damned were punk's...what? Clowns? Court jesters? Pariahs? Where the Pistols preached anarchy and The Clash advocated bloody revolution, The Damned seemed to have no ambition beyond the next line of speed and the next pint of lager. "We want to have some fun and make a lot of money," said drummer Rat Scabies. "I've been poor all my life, I want a big house, a big car and a big colour TV. And so does everyone else if they're honest."

The Damned first formed under the name Masters Of The Backside. This was an idea of Sex Pistol's manager Malcolm McLaren. Chrissie Hynde (later to find fame with The Pretenders) was supposed to dress as a boy and whip the rest of the band while they played. Not surprisingly, Masters Of The Backside never made it to the stage of actually playing a gig.

The Damned spread chaos and anger wherever they went. They attacked the other punk bands verbally in the press – and sometimes physically when they met. Their live shows passed in a blur of speed, noise and spitting.

They had a lead singer called Dave Vanian – a former grave digger who dressed like a charity shop version of a Hammer Horror Count Dracula. And they had a bassist called Captain Sensible – a former toilet cleaner who often performed dressed in a ballet tutu or as a female nurse. And, in guitarist Brian James, they also had a brilliant songwriter.

"New Rose" was the first UK punk record. It was made, admits Captain Sensible, in a blitzkrieg of cider, adrenaline and amphetamine sulphate. And it sounds like it. The Damned play as if they have a mortal dread that the world might explode in the next three minutes.

"New Rose" starts with a plaintive, almost naïve, "Is she really going out with him?" And this is answered by one of the most sensational, thundering drum intros ever. Thereafter the song crashes around like a gang of speed-addled drunks in a china shop. It is distilled chaos. It was drunken yob punk's first inarticulate scream. It is, says Jon Savage, "the first bulletin from an accelerated age". And it is a love song.

A pure and simple and quite lovely love song. Performed by maniacs.

Neat Neat Neat

This, released in February of 1977, was The Damned's second single – released at a time when most of their Brit punk contemporaries hadn't even made it into the studio. And it remains The Damned's finest moment.

NEW ROSE / HELP!
SINGLE. STIFF. 1976

NEAT NEAT NEAT / STAB YOR
BACK / SINGALONGA SCABIES
SINGLE. STIFF. 1977

Dead Boys
Sonic Reducer

Originally from Cleveland, Ohio, the Dead Boys moved to New York and soon became stalwarts of the CBGB's scene. The focal point of the band was Stiv Bators, a ferret-faced, whippet-thin exhibitionist who mutilated and hung himself during shows. Stiv's other on-stage tricks included vomiting and receiving blowjobs from members of the audience. The Dead Boys apparently got their record deal with Sire records by mooning future label-mates The Ramones from the roof of a speeding car.

The Dead Boys were not nice. Influenced both by the "garage rock" of Iggy Pop And The Stooges and by British punk bands like the Sex Pistols, the Dead Boys seemed determined to outpunk every other band in

Despite their vulgar image, the Dead Boys were partial to a well-made pina colada.

New York. They revelled in nihilism, ugliness, vulgarity and violence. They scrawled swastikas and slogans such as "Hitler was right" on their guitar cases – and that's not very nice at all, is it? And they rocked.

"Sonic Reducer" is the opening track of their 1977 album *Young, Loud And Snotty*. The song had been written by guitarist Cheetah Chrome (who, along with Dave Thomas, would later go on to found art-rock band Pere Ubu) back when he and Stiv has been in a Cleveland band called Rocket From The Tombs.

Cheetah Chrome remembers: "In 1975, Rocket From The Tombs rehearsed practically every weeknight at our loft on West 6th Street in Cleveland. Sometimes a couple of us would get there earlier than the others and usually we'd use that time to run ideas by each other. One night Crocus had the lyrics to 'Reducer' and this keyboard intro, with sort of a chant thing. I read them over a couple of times, picked up my guitar, and the riff just came out. It didn't take 10 minutes. I've always considered the RFTT version to be the 'official' version, so the Dead Boys version was really a cover, even though it came out 27 years before the RFTT version!"

The Dead Boys were always too mentalist to hit the big time and never really received the attention they deserved, but "Sonic Reducer" remains an all-time punk classic. Shame about the swastikas, though.

And, finally, here's a bit of advice for the youth of today from Cheetah Chrome: "Think for yourself, always question authority, and don't settle for less. And LIMP BIZKIT IS NOT ROCK AND ROLL!!!!!"

YOUNG, LOUD AND SNOTTY ALBUM. SIRE. 1977

Dead Kennedys

California Uber Alles

"Isn't a Dead Kennedys concert on 22 November [anniversary of JFK's assassination] in rather bad taste?"
"Of course. But the assassinations weren't too tasteful either."

Dead Kennnedys guitarist East Bay Ray interviewed in 1979 by the *Vancouver Sun*

Dead Kennedys singer Jello Biafra was/is a paranoid genius, and it was his melodramatic Orwellian lyrics – delivered in a curious, warbling, high-pitched nasal whine – that helped make the Dead Kennedys the outstanding US punk band of the post-Ramones generation.

The young Biafra wanted to grow up to be a Batman villain – and that's more than apparent in the sardonically grinning, Joker-like stage persona that Biafra adopted to ram his message home. Whereas most punk bands attacked their targets head on, the Kennedys tended to use a more subtle approach. Often Biafra would adopt the voice of the target of his own hatred – the rich landlord, the arrogant yuppie, the corrupt politician – as he did on what is widely (and correctly) regarded as their third best song, "Kill The Poor". He wasn't the first to do this. The Irish satirist Jonathan Swift (author of *Gulliver's Travels*) had made a similar point in 1729 when, in an essay titled *A Modest Proposal*, he suggested that the poor eat their own children.

Biafra knew this, of course. Whereas many punk bands pretended to be as dumb as bricks (and, let's be honest, there were many punk bands who actually were as dumb as bricks), the Kennedys were always about education and empowerment. Not for nothing have they been described as "the American Clash".

Like Oi! and anarcho-punk, US hardcore punk had evolved partly in reaction to what was seen as the increasing commercialization and "softening" of the original UK punk bands. But for some critics, these new branches of punk threw the baby out with the bathwater. Hardcore was fast and brutal and confrontational, but where was the wit, the humour, the sense of fun?

In many respects the Dead Kennedys provided the link between US hardcore's determination to "get back to basics" and UK punk's sense of playful theatricality. This latter, of course, had its roots in the 1960s – with the Situationists who'd taken part in the Paris street riots of 1968 and with the American "yippies" who nominated a pig for president and even attempted to "levitate" the White House.

This influence was apparent when, in 1984, the band appeared on stage wearing Klan hoods, which they removed to reveal Ronald Reagan masks. That same year Biafra led a mob that screamed "Fuck off and die!" at delegates to the Republican convention in Dallas.

Above all, the Kennedys sought confrontation – and they got it. In 1986 Biafra was arrested for the heinous crime of "distributing harmful matter to minors". The harmful matter was a poster by Oscar-winning *Alien* artist HR Geiger that had been given away with the Kennedys' album *Frankenchrist*. Called *Penis Landscape*, the Geiger artwork appeared to show rows of penises stuck into rows of anuses, with both organs and orifices fused into one hideously unnatural organic whole.

Biafra claimed it was "a metaphor for consumer society". The authorities just thought it was disgusting. The long, dragged-out court case became a cause célèbre for the US hardcore punk scene, and it was fought out against the background of a rising moral panic about rock and rap music that was largely orchestrated by Christian fundamentalist preachers and a group of busybody Washington politicians' wives called the Parents' Music Resource Center (PMRC).

Unsurprisingly, these folks just didn't get songs like "Kill The Poor" (it's actually an anti-neutron bomb song – duh!). Former LA deputy city attorney Michael Guarino later admitted: "About midway through the trial, we realized that the lyrics of the album were in many ways socially responsible – very anti-drug and pro-individual." Like, DUH!

Biafra stood as the Green Party candidate in the 2000 US presidential elections, but this wasn't his first bid for office. In 1979, shortly after he'd joined the Kennedys, Biafra ran for mayor of San Francisco. Among his many slogans were "Apocalypse now – vote Biafra", "If he doesn't win I'll kill myself" and "There's always room for Jello". He came fourth out of ten candidates.

1979 was also the year that the Dead Kennedys released their first single, "California Uber Alles". It was and remains an amazing piece of music. It is an hysterical (in every meaning of the word) and totally over-the-top attack on then-California Governor Jerry Brown.

The song, says Biafra, is about the "post-WWII baby boom" generation. The generation that had discovered free love and protested against racism, environmental degradation and the Vietnam War in the 1960s but was now, for the first time, finding itself in positions of real political power.

By the early '70s, says Biafra, a lot of the people who had been radicalized in the 1960s "had just gotten to the point of – Where do I go from here?" And were coming up with the answer "that there was nothing there! It was kind of hollow, and so a lot of people seemed to be wanting to be told what to do – that's one more of the reasons why you see more and more people turning to totalitarian mindfuck organizations."

Southern California in the late 1970s was home to a large number of pseudo-religious organizations, all of whom associated themselves with the leftist-libertarianism of the 1960s while at the same time imposing on their members a discipline that did indeed smack of fascism.

In Biafra's extremely active (some would say paranoid) imagination, this was projected forward into a vision of an imminent hippie-fascist super-state, where the worst excesses of the nazis would be committed by a new,

laidback and superficially groovy southern Californian hippie Gestapo.

"California Uber Alles" managed to combine punk's fear of an authoritarian future (The Clash's "English Civil War") with its tendency to see elements of fascism within consumerism (the Sex Pistols' "Holidays In The Sun") and with its cynical and sneering mistrust of the previous generation of troublemaking folk devils – the hippies. And the result is an all-time, stand-out, paranoid-punk classic.

When the single was released in the UK, the Kennedys (who were still almost totally unknown in the States) became an overnight sensation and a punk legend was born. Through their music and through their label, Alternative Tentacles, the Dead Kennedys helped spread the hardcore scene throughout the industrialized world – at the exact same time as the music press in London and New York were declaring that punk was dead.

Holiday In Cambodia

Thematically similar but lyrically superior to the Sex Pistols' brilliant "Holidays In The Sun", "Holiday In Cambodia" is the musical equivalent of an episode of *The Twilight Zone*.

Between 1975 and 1978, an estimated two million people died in Cambodia. They were victims of the brutal Khmer Rouge regime that, under the leadership of Pol Pot, managed to destroy a staggering 21 per cent of the county's entire population.

Despite the allegedly Marxist origins of the Khmer Rouge, Pol Pot was backed by the US government. This was because the Khmer Rouge were at war with Vietnam (with whom America had recently lost a war). When the Vietnamese army eventually liberated Cambodia, the world reacted with disbelieving horror at the evidence of genocide.

The entire urban population had been force-marched into the fields. Many thousands were executed on the spot. Possessing a pair of spectacles was enough to mark you as an "intellectual" (and thus deserving of a

"America's answer to The Clash" – the Dead Kennedys.

Jello Biafra begs the audience to return his T-shirt.

bullet in the back of the neck). The rest were forced to work for up to 15 hours a day in slave labour conditions. Hundreds of thousands were worked and starved to death in the now infamous "killing fields".

Meanwhile, in America, a new stereotype was emerging. The "yuppie" (an acronym of "young, upwardly mobile professional") would come to symbolize 1980s America every bit as much as the "hippie" had the 1960s.

This new breed of dynamic, thrusting, get-ahead young executives would buy into the Reagan dream wholesale. Not surprisingly, the punks saw the yuppies as the enemy and mocked and vilified the sold-out sons-of-bitches in countless songs.

But no one did it as well as or as viciously (or early) as the Dead Kennedys. In "Holiday" Biafra mocks the spoilt little rich kid (the actual term "yuppie" wouldn't be invented for at least another three years) who has no real contact whatsoever with impoverished, working-class or black America – and yet patronizingly claims an affinity with its earthiness, with its authenticity, with its "soul".

And then, in a demented and utterly malicious leap of imagination, the upper-class "wigga" (another word that had yet to be invented) finds himself suddenly transported to the killing fields of Cambodia "where people dress in black/ A holiday in Cambodia – where you'll kiss ass or crack."

Yeah! That'll learn 'em!

CALIFORNIA UBER ALLES /
THE MAN WITH THE DOGS
SINGLE. ALTERNATIVE
TENTACLES. 1979

HOLIDAY IN CAMBODIA /
POLICE TRUCK
SINGLE. IRS. 1980

The Descendents
Suburban Home

Do you like Greenday, punk? Well, do ya? Well, here's where the whole snotty, petulant, don't-wanna-grow-up three-minute cry-baby loser-punk thing started. In fact, once you've heard "Suburban Home", you're never going to see "Dookie" in the same light again (and the same goes for all you Good Charlotte, Sum 41 and Blink 182 fans).

Punk "hard men" Johnny Rotten and Sid Vicious were widely regarded as satanically inspired shocktroops of unbridled chaos and mindless anarchy, but the truth is that they were a couple of awkward, nerdy and sexually frustrated adolescents who were only *pretending* to be satanically inspired shocktroops of unbridled chaos and mindless anarchy (in fact, they were both living with their mums when they joined the Sex Pistols).

The Descendents were nerds who wrote songs for other nerds about what it's like to be a nerd. They articulated the viewpoint of the geek with the glasses. When other bands were singing about anarchy or revolution, The Descendents were fixated on coffee, food and girls. They were an American high-school version of England's Jilted John, with a couple of nods in the direction of The Buzzcocks and The Ramones thrown in for good measure.

The truth is, of course, that punk was the nerd's music. It attracted losers, weirdoes and the socially maladjusted the way shit attracts flies. But, once in a band, the kid with no cool friends was free to reinvent him or herself. They could be whatever the hell they wanted to be! They could become the Incredible Hulk – like Henry Rollins out of Black Flag. They could become society's worst nightmare – like the Sex Pistols. Or street-sussed revolutionaries – like The Clash. Or mentally subnormal pinheads – like The Ramones.

The Descendents, however, opted for honesty, and they set about making nerdiness the new gold standard for cool. While it might be putting it a tad too strongly to claim that they actually invented "pop punk", they certainly pioneered the US branch of a sub-genre that (for better or worse) is still going strong today.

The Descendents did not take themselves too seriously. In fact, they didn't take themselves seriously at all. "Suburban Home" is just one of the kick-ass tracks off their never-to-be surpassed 1982 album *Milo Goes To College* (so-called because singer Milo Aukerman was indeed about to go off to college).

"I want to be stereotyped…I want to be a clone," drones Milo like a lobotomized robot. There is real sarcastic anger here, aimed at the jocks and homecoming queens whose sole ambition in life is to build "a suburban home" just "like mom and dad", and as such it will still strike a chord with anybody who's been through the American high-school system and sided with the despised outsiders (rather than the pampered high-flyers, the spoilt sports superstars and the future Stepford Wives).

This, of course, is a subject that has been dealt with elsewhere – in *Buffy* and in the movies *Heathers* and *Revenge Of The Nerds* – but never with such sarcastic savagery. Or with such a great tune.

MILO GOES TO COLLEGE ALBUM. NEW ALLIANCE RECORDS. 1982

Desperate Bicycles
Advice On Arrest

"It was the Desperate Bicycles that gave us the incentive. 'If you're thinking of making a tape why not go the whole way and make a record?' they said."

Scritti Politti, *Sounds* magazine, January 1979

Ask the average person to define punk rock and they'll probably tell you it's kinda like heavy metal but faster and a bit more political. This, of course, is bollocks. And it doesn't even start to describe the almost demented variety of weird and wonderful singles that came out on the independent labels that mushroomed almost overnight in Britain in the wake of the Sex Pistols.

Nowadays the word "indie" is used to describe the music made by any guitar band but, in 1977 and for good few years after, there were literally thousands of tiny, independent punk labels. Some put out one single and sank without trace (with the unsold singles stacked under the singer's bed for years after). Others, like Fast records (who released singles by The Mekons, Gang Of 4, Delta 5, The Redskins, Newtown Neurotics and even released the Dead Kennedys' "California Uber Alles" in the UK), grew and flourished.

DIY (do-it-yourself) took on a life of its own. There were even those who argued that DIY punk was the only real punk, and that the bands that had signed to the majors (like the Sex Pistols and The Clash) were mercenary sellouts who had become the very thing they had set out to destroy.

The point was that punk's message that ANYBODY could make a record/be a star was taken literally by thousands of kids all over the UK. Suddenly, 90 per cent of all the most exciting music in the world was being made in bedrooms (or in garages or grotty provincial recording studios) and packaged in cheaply printed sleeves. Or, in some cases, just slung in a brown paper bag with the song details scrawled on the front in marker pen.

This demented level of activity couldn't last. The major labels rushed around signing up any and all punk bands that they suspected of having even the slightest chance of actually being commercial. But the DIY ethic survived (and is still going strong today). When British punk finally spluttered to a near-halt in the 1980s, the baton had already been passed on to the hardcore punk scene in the US.

It was in America that DIY punk found the space to breathe and survive. Although they speak the same language (sort of), the British and the Americans have always had a radically different attitude towards music. The British music industry has been compared to an experimental lab hidden away in the back of the massive American music factory. In this lab new experiments are always being carried out, and these experiments often throw up weird and wonderful results – like punk. But Britain is a small and crowded country. Movements like punk have got nowhere to hide. As soon as anything radical or exciting appears, the British record companies descend like wolves. The radical can become the mainstream in a matter of months.

So in Britain – probably more than in any country in the world – musical fashions flash by at an amazing rate. By the start of the 1980s punk was already considered old-fashioned. The once madly enthusiastic music press had moved on to sing the praises of the distinctly un-punky "new romantics" and would soon be championing the dispirited and defeatist whining of a band called The Smiths.

But in America, with its massively larger population and geographical size, an underground movement like punk could grow at its own pace, on its own terms and under its own rules – and be almost entirely ignored by the major labels. That's why the punk DIY ethic took root and flourished in the US long after it had all but withered and died in the UK.

Ian Mackaye from US hardcore legends Fugazi remembers: "There was no industry in Washington DC. No one else was going to put our music out, so we decided that we'd just start our own label, a label that was going to document what was happening in Washington DC. We had the idea that you were supposed to strike out on your own and make things happen.

"It took us about three or four months to figure out how to make a record. We took singles from England and carefully pried the sleeve apart to see how it was constructed, then we traced the unfolded sleeve and laid our artwork inside the outline...then using scissors we cut, folded and glued every sleeve of our first 10,000 records."

The two records that started this DIY avalanche back in the UK were "Spiral Scratch" by The Buzzcocks and "Smokescreen" from the Desperate Bicycles. For Manchester's Buzzcocks, DIY was a means to an end (they soon signed to a major label), but for the Desperate Bicycles (who chose their name because they were "desperate for equipment"), DIY was the very reason for their existence. Many of their songs were about telling other people how to put their own records out. Their second release featured the song "The Medium Is Tedium", which had the chorus: "It was easy/ It was cheap, go and do it." On the flip side was "Don't Back The Front", with its slogan: "Cut it, press it, distribute it/ Xerox music is here to stay."

And people did. Although almost no one remembers them now, the Desperate Bicycles were one of most incredibly influential punk bands ever. Many other groups – including Scritti Politti and Alternative TV – have admitted that it was the Bicycles that inspired them to put their own singles out instead of just waiting for a major record company to show interest. Without DIY, punk might have been just another flash-in-the pan pop phenomenon. And without Desperate Bicycles, DIY would never have taken on its passionate ideological nature – and it is quite possible that the US hardcore explosion would never have happened.

"Advice On Arrest" comes from the Bicycles' *New Cross, New Cross* EP. It is pure and simple punk (with not a crashing guitar or an angry, snarling vocal in earshot). Whereas The Clash mythologized their own occasional confrontations with the forces of law and order ("Guns On The Roof", "White Riot"), the Bicycles typically take a more practical approach and tell the listening punk what to do (should he or she ever be grabbed by the fuzz).

Over the next few decades thousands of punk bands would write thousands of songs about the police – usually saying how horrid the cops are – but none of them would be as useful as "Advice On Arrest". And without the Desperate Bicycles, it is entirely possible that many of those punk bands wouldn't have existed in the first place.

NEW CROSS, NEW CROSS EP. REFILL. MAY 1978

Devo modelling a look that would later be ripped off by Backstreet Boys.

Devo

Jocko Homo

"Are we not men? We are Devo…"

Were Devo punk? Were they even human? They dressed like 1950s scientists, danced like robots and, according to rock writer Gary Mulholland, played "off-kilter, nerd-celebrating electronic rock that oozed disgust for the consumerism, machismo and nostalgia of modern America". Gee, sounds kinda punky to me.

Devo were one of those punk bands that didn't play punk rock. They were weird. And they were punk because they were weird and didn't play punk rock. Does that make sense? Far too many bands thought the idea behind punk was to look and sound as much like the Sex Pistols or Black Flag as possible. Devo never made that mistake. They made a completely different mistake. They looked and sounded like Martians who, having just beamed down, thought they'd have a go at this thing the earthlings call pop music. Yeah, they were punk.

"Jocko Homo", the band's 1977 debut single, is about the philosophy of devolution. What is devolution? Well, it's kinda about how modern technology and the consumer society is turning us all into something akin to the Borg outa *Star Trek*. And how we all leave emptier lives than any previous generation of humans. And how time is slowing down and going into reverse. Or something.

The ideas behind devolution (that would eventually inform the lyrics of "Jocko Homo") first came to band member Jerry Casale on 4 May 1970 when he was a student at Kent State University, Ohio. On that day national guardsmen opened fire on students who were peacefully protesting against the Vietnam War. And Casale was there.

"All I can tell you is that it completely and utterly changed my life," he told Brian L Knight of the *Vermont Review*. "I was a white hippie boy and then I saw exit wounds from M1 rifles out of the backs of two people I knew. Two of the four people who were killed, Jeffrey Miller and Allison Krause, were my friends. We were all running our asses off from these motherfuckers. It was total utter bullshit. They shot into a crowd that was running. I stopped being a hippie and I started to develop the idea of devolution. I got real, real pissed off.

"Until then I was a hippie. I thought that the world is essentially good. If people were evil, there was justice and that the law mattered. All of those silly naïve things. I saw the depths of the horrors and lies and the evil." You know what? I'd say Devo were *definitely* punks.

Q: ARE WE NOT MEN?
A: WE ARE DEVO
ALBUM. WARNER BROS
(STIFF IN THE UK). 1978

The Distillers

The World Comes Tumblin'

"Start a riot, slash ya wrists red/ you want an answer?"

"I spit on the whole fucking celebrity side of this business," snarls Distillers singer/guitarist Brody Armstrong.

You've probably noticed that most of the bands in this book are from punk's so-called golden age (roughly 1975–1989), but with The Distillers we come bang up to date. I make no apologies. The Distillers are fantastic and they remain one of the best live bands I have ever seen (and I've been going to punk shows since 1977).

Brody Armstrong wasn't even born when *Never Mind The Bollocks* came out. Hailing from Melbourne, Australia, she started her first band, the all-girl Sourpuss, at age 14. They rehearsed at a place called Rock'n'Roll High School that, claims Brody, was run by "psychotic feminist nazi sows".

She grew up, moved to America, married Tim Armstrong (lead singer with punk band Rancid – the two are no longer together) and made one of the greatest punk albums ever, the eponymous *The Distillers*.

On it you can hear all of Brody's oft-listed influences – Discharge, Black Flag, The Ramones and Blondie. And you can also hear Rancid, and through Rancid the clanging, rushing, garbled glory of the early Clash. It is a sensational record, but one that is as much overlooked by 1970s- and '80s-obsessed punk fans as the great Rancid album *And Out Come The Wolves*.

Any one of half a dozen tracks from that record could have made it into this book. The album catches The Distillers at their furious, frenzied best. Over a melodic riot Brody growls more than sings, coming across like Pattie Smith with rabies. The Distillers are definitely a punk band – the deranged haircuts, lurid tattoos and menacing "fuck you" 'tude would tell you that, even before you'd heard them play a note – but they are also a great rock'n'roll band. And like all the great rock'n'rollers, they've assembled a sound that constantly reminds you of past glories but never sounds nostalgic, tired or retro.

The Distillers, basically, have got "it" – that elusive combination of energy, self-belief, passion and talent that marks the great out from the also-rans. Nobody who has ever seen them live could possibly doubt that. And anybody reading this who thinks punk in the 21st century starts and finishes with young, dumb Sum 41, really – seriously – needs to check them out.

"World Comes Tumblin'" (which, by the way, has one of the best choruses of any rock song ever) is about the depressing futility of self-mutilation. The song name-checks a girl called Gerti Rouge (Gerti appears in several Distillers songs). "That's not her real name," Armstrong explained to Judith Lewis of *LA Weekly* magazine in 2003, "but she's my childhood best friend, and she was molested by her father since age zero until she was about 14. Her mother was a child psychologist, which made the situation even sicker. In the '80s her mom was just addicted to pills, and knew what was going on but didn't know how to stop it. She was obese, and just fed her pain and fed her guilt.

"When me and my mom took her out of that situation, we told her mother what was going on, and her mother came over to my house. I was sitting there, and her mother pulled out a clipboard, and instead of holding her child she just asked, 'So, tell me what happened?' And Gerti's sitting there crying. My mother was so disgusted. It was so fucking unbelievable. We were like: 'This is your child, not someone else's child.' It was unfuckingbelievable."

THE DISTILLERS ALBUM. HELLCAT. 2000

Brody Armstrong – full of "fuck you" 'tude.

Eddie And The Hot Rods
Do Anything You Wanna Do

"The first time I ever heard the word 'punk' used to describe anything that anyone was doing was in *Time Out,* a London listings magazine, where they said: 'Eddie And The Hot Rods is the second generation of punk bands.' I remember reading this and going – What is this punk? What is this word?"

Clash singer Joe Strummer, in an interview on The Clash's *Westway To The World* DVD

In *Bower,* a book about being a punk-loving football hooligan in the English city of Bristol in the 1970s, Chris Brown writes: "If I needed any further convincing that my love affair with dance music was over, the 'Rods released 'Do Anything You Wanna Do'...Forget the spitting and the pogoing, forget the bizarre fashion and Malcolm McLaren's posturing. This record more than any other summed up what punk was all about."

But in London the nasty new leather-jacketed music journalists and the coterie of freaks, poseurs and wannabes that hung around the Sex Pistols firmly denied that Eddie And The Hot Rods were punk at all. The Rods had been involved in the previously popular "pub rock" scene and were thus tainted.

Mind you, so had Joe Strummer of The Clash. But the Rods had also made the fatal mistake of pissing off the Sex Pistols by sacking the band from a tour after they'd trashed the Rods' equipment. And so, the "proper" punks were adamant, Eddie And The Hot Rods were just a bunch of bandwagon-jumping hippie wankers.

Aw, who cares? "Do Anything You Wanna Do" (complete with its corny "disco" handclaps) summed up what it was like to be young, punked up and living in England in 1977. The lyrics aren't poetry, the music isn't exactly avant-garde and the band definitely look like they could do with a haircut – but so what? Who cares? We didn't. Nobody outside of London did. Out in "the provinces" we were flying on the punk energy that was buzzing and crackling all around us. And here's a record that sums it all up – dumbly and precisely. It's a punk classic – and the snobs and the purists can kiss my (now wrinkled) provincial punk arse.

DO ANYTHING YOU WANNA DO / SCHOOLGIRL LOVE SINGLE. ISLAND. 1977

Long hair and flared trousers – but Eddie And The Hot Rods were still a punk band.

Elastica

Stutter

"Debbie Harry was the first girl I fell in love with"

Elastica's Justine Frischmann

The mid-'90s saw a clutch of new punky bands getting a lot of music press attention in the UK. Labelled the "new wave of new wave", these bands looked back to The Buzzcocks and Blondie in much the same way that their Britpop compatriots (like Oasis and Blur) looked back to The Beatles and the Small Faces.

The "new wave of new wave" band that stood out from all the rest was Elastica. Their eponymous debut album was an absolute killer. It was packed with top 1977-style pop tunes, and if they "borrowed" more than a few of their riffs from The Stranglers, Wire and Blondie, so what? It's what they did with those riffs that matters.

Kings and queens of the "new wave of new wave" – Elastica.

Justine Frischmann, Elastica's singer, has a haunting, rather posh and distinctively disinterested voice. It was as if the cool and refined lady of the manor had one day decided to give fox-hunting a miss and try her hand at punk rock instead. Which was cool, because Justine was posh and she really *couldn't* give a fuck. And she had a *wicked* way with a punk rock tune (all frantically bashed drums, thundering bass and clanging, chiming guitars).

"Stutter" is about the things women tell men when the men are too drunk to fuck. It's funny (if you're female) and scary (if you're male). And it has got to be one of the best punk songs about sex (or the lack of it) ever recorded. Justine, by the way, was going out with Damon Albarn, lead singer of Britpop band Blur, at the time. This might or might not be a coincidence.

ELASTICA ALBUM. DECEPTIVE. 1995

77–EARLY YEARS–79
ALBUM. STEP FORWARD.
1981

The Fall
Rowche Rumble

The Fall were great. They were working class but as arty as hell. Led by a pinch-faced Manchester misanthrope called Mark E Smith who moaned more than he sang, The Fall took disco, rock'n'roll, rockabilly, fairground organ, surf music and anything else they could find and threw it into their eclectic and decidedly eccentric punk rock stew.

The most fascinating thing about Mark E Smith is that he just kept going – whether punk was fashionable or not, whether The Fall were selling any records or not and whether he'd just once again sacked everybody else in the band or not. In fact, The Fall are still going strong today. And all this time Mark has maintained his image as the "gobshite" working-class bloke who just happens to be in a rock band. And who just happens to keep putting out weird and totally out-there punk records that make most of the stuff labelled "avant-garde" look as dull and as uninteresting as yesterday's fish'n'chip wrappers.

There is a legend that surrounds 1979's "Rowche Rumble". Mark was working as a clerk for a shipping firm. One day he found to his horror that he had a huge surplus of anti-depressants (manufactured by the Swiss drug company Roche).

"I send 70 pounds instead of 70 p [slang for 'pence'] to pharmaceutical company Rowche AG/ The lorry arrived the next day…" The song tells the tale of the young Mr Smith's frantic and increasingly desperate attempts to hide the drugs from his boss. What is he going to do with all those pills? Will he get away with it or will he be rumbled? (It'd make a great movie.)

On another level, "Rowche Rumble" is about the demented hypocrisy of a society that condemns "drugs" while, at the same time, doctors hand out millions of little white pills to women whose only real problem is probably the fact that they lead incredibly dull and uninteresting lives.

The Rolling Stones made this point first in their song "Mother's Little Helper". But The Fall did it better.

A very early picture of The Fall's Mark E Smith – by heck, he was pretty!

Fear
I Love Living In The City

For many people the word "punk" has always been interchangeable with the phrase "dirty, disgusting, drunken, loudmouth yob", and Fear did their darndest to prove those people right.

Fear were southern Californian hardcore punk originals. Their totally over-the-top mentalist nihilism drove away many people before they had a chance to realize that Fear were actually a shit-hot punk rock band. They had a drummer called Spit, a bassist called Derf Scratch (catchphrase – "Eat my fuck!") and songs entitled "Fuck Authority", "Fuck Xmas", "Bomb The Russians" and "The Mouth Don't Stop (The Trouble With Women Is)".

Drummer Spit Stix sums up Fear thus: "Plenty of people thought our stage rantings were serious. Dead Kennedys thought we were fascists. Homophobes thought we were gay. Lesbians thought we were misogynists. Entertainment is a form of employment. We were just working hard."

So what is their most famous song, "I Love Living In The City", about? It is, of course, a celebration of the heart-warming brotherly love to be found whenever and wherever human beings gather to live in peace, love and harmony.

The air smells shitty. There's pools of puke and blood. Piles of scabs and hair. And the bodies of dead and dying junkies. "But the suburban scumbags, they don't care/ Just get fat and dye their hair…"

"I Love Living In The City" was not adopted as the anthem of the Californian tourist board.

Strange, that.

I LOVE LIVING IN THE CITY / NOW YOU'RE DEAD SINGLE. CRIMINAL. 1978

Gang Of Four
At Home He's A Tourist

The Gang Of Four have been massively influential. You can add U2, Rage Against The Machine, Korn and Limp Bizkit to the list of bands that would all have sounded radically different if the world had never heard the Gang's strange mix of Wilko Johnson meets Jimi Hendrix guitar and "perverted disco" bass lines.

Formed in the northern English city of Leeds in 1977, the Gang Of Four were the most political, articulate and educated of all the old-school UK punk bands. And boy were they political. Ex-art students, the Gang were heavily influenced by the writings of the feminist Griselda Pollock and former Situationist and socialist art historian TJ Clark.

But the biggest influence on the Gang Of Four (after, perhaps, soul legend James Brown and pub rockers Dr Feelgood) was Karl Marx, the 19th-century German philosopher regarded today as "the father of communism".

But don't let this blind you to the fact that the Gang Of Four fucking rocked. They were no ivory tower eggheads. In 1977 Leeds – like most British cities – was a violent place. Bassist Dave Allen and singer John King met at an anti-fascist rally where King was beaten up by the police. Drummer Hugo Burnham became something

"Gang Of Four knew how to swing. I stole a lot from them."

Michael Stipe (REM)

"Gang Of Four is the first rock band I could truly relate to... These Limeys rocked my world."

Flea (Red Hot Chili Peppers)

of a legend among the left-wing Leeds punks when nazi thugs attacked the pub he was drinking in. According to eyewitnesses, Burnham quietly finished his pint, zipped up his jacket and then waded into the nazis, both fists working overtime.

At an early gig the profoundly anti-sexist group discovered that they'd been booked to play on the same stage as a stripper. The woman explained to them: "You know, we're both in the entertainment business, we have to give the audience what they want. I don't like to do this but I earn double the amount I'd get if I were in a nine-to-five job."

When the Gang Of Four released their first record (the *Damaged Goods* EP that features "At Home He's A Tourist"), it featured a photo of a female bullfighter on the cover.

"You know, we're both in the entertainment business..." says the matador.

"I think that at some point we have to take responsibility for our actions," replies the bull.

The clever stuff didn't finish with the sleeve. "At Home He's A Tourist" was about alienation – the idea that human beings were "de-natured" by capitalism, and that capitalism has taken over and fucked up all aspects of our lives – including our sex lives. It's also about the Marxist concept of "commodity fetishism", which is about the way humans under capitalism give value to stuff that's basically just crap (gold being a good example, U2 records being another).

Now this might all sound like airy-fairy intellectual bollocks but the reality is that the Gang Of Four were actually singing about the same things as a lot of other punk groups. It was just that the Gang could back it up with the hardcore theory in interviews. You've also got to remember that the record came out at a time when a lot of working-class and relatively poorly educated kids were turning to punk for all sorts of answers. This aspect of punk, its ability to lead its audience on to learn about all kinds of other stuff, was summed up years later by the Manic Street Preachers when they said "the library was our university". And, godamn it, so were our record collections.

The true genius of the Gang Of Four was their ability to take intellectual or abstract concepts like fetishism or

The Gang Of Four ponder infinity...or possibly a passing pigeon.

"The early Gang Of Four line-up made some of the greatest and most influential music of the last fifteen years."

Page Hamilton (Helmut)

"(They) took no prisoners. It was art meets the devil via James Brown."

Michael Hutchence (INXS)

alienation and reduce them down to smart, cutting punk lyrics. And, as I've already said, they fucking rocked.

In the sleeve notes for the Gang Of Four compilation album, *A Hundred Flowers Bloom*, rock critic Jon Savage writes: "What you get with Gang Of Four records is nothing less than a world-class hard rock/funk band capable of inspiring audiences and musicians alike; there are few moments in rock more thrilling than...the uptight, visceral urgency of 'At Home He's A Tourist'. Once you get past this surface, should you wish to, you find the lyrics – a brilliant sequence of prophetic, staccato aphorisms that stick in your mind like a burr and make you see the world in a new way."

As brilliant as "Tourist" was, it reached a whole new level of notoriety (always a good thing for a punk record) when the BBC (the UK's semi-official broadcasting organization) banned it. The lines that caused all the trouble were: "And the rubbers you hide/ In your top left pocket."

The BBC demanded that the Gang Of Four change the word "rubbers" to "rubbish" before they'd let them appear on Britain's primetime TV music show, *Top Of The Pops*.

Guitarist Andy Gill remembers: "We said – Fuck it, OK! So we went off and changed it to 'packets'. We thought it was fine. But they told us – No, we want you to use the word 'rubbish' so that it's less obvious that there's been a change, a censorship...I think at that point we told them to shove it. To tell you the truth, I think they were trying to get that reaction so that we wouldn't go on the show. They felt we were a bit too extreme for them all around."

They were probably right.

DAMAGED GOODS
EP. FAST. 1978

AT HOME HE'S A TOURIST /
IT'S HER FACTORY
SINGLE. EMI. 1979

Generation X

King Rocker

> ## "Little William Broad was a big tosser even then, before he started calling himself Billy Idol. We used to call him the punk Cliff Richard, because that's what we thought he looked like. When Generation X were playing, we'd all be throwing shit at them, because even then, Billy Idol was a wanker."

Gareth Holder (The Shapes)

Bleached-blond pretty boy Billy Idol was one of the young punks who hung around with the Sex Pistols in the early days – the so-called Bromley Contingent. All these kids had plans. They were all going to be famous, but little did they suspect that, out of all of them, it would be gorgeous but slightly goofy Billy who would go on to become a world-famous pop idol.

Before Billy became one of the biggest mainstream rock stars of the 1980s, he was lead singer in Generation X. Generation X didn't give a shit about the Pistol's anarchy or The Clash's righteousness. They were about pop art and glamour. None of the hardcore punks took Generation X at all seriously, of course, but that didn't stop them from making some great records.

"King Rocker" is probably the best of a fantastic bunch. Generation X weren't earthshakers or groundbreakers. They didn't want to burn rock's mansion down and build something truer and more beautiful in the ashes. To hell with that, they wanted to *be* rock stars!

> ## "Jailhouse Rocker roots training down/ In Memphis"

Generation X were in love with Elvis. They were in love with The Beatles and the Rolling Stones. They looked like punks. They snarled and swaggered and sneered like punks. They even sounded like punks. They were born right at the centre of the whole UK punk scene. Somehow, though, they just didn't get it. But that didn't really matter. They crashed into the mainstream charts

in a blur of peroxide and cheekbones and took the punk 'tude to millions of kids who would also dream of becoming king rockers. They sold the idea – brilliantly and beautifully – that pop music should be short, sharp, aggressive, glamorous and made in a perpetually excited rush. And that was enough.

**GENERATION X
SINGLE. CHRYSALIS. 1978**

Beautiful but gormless – Billy Idol of Generation X.

The Germs
What We Do Is Secret

Germs frontman Darby Crash was US punk's answer to Sid Vicious and he had the self-destructive attitude to match – live fast and die young in a black leather jacket (after offending as many people as possible on the way). And he did exactly that, overdosing on heroin at the grand old age of 22.

With Crash on vocals and Pat Smear (later of Nirvana and the Foo Fighters) on guitar, the Germs' twisted and brutal punk was a major influence on West Coast US hardcore. Their messy sound was even more chaotic than that of their Brit counterparts like the Sex Pistols, Clash or Damned. The Pistols always claimed they couldn't play their instruments. The Germs *really* struggled, regularly playing out of tune and out of time at live shows, but it all added to the recklessness and snotty nihilism that made The Germs so thrilling.

"What We Do Is Secret" is a characteristic Germs blast of satisfyingly shambolic confusion that paved the way for the hardcore sound that would soon come to dominate the Californian punk scene. It clocks in at (a you-better-be-fucking-paying-attention) 45 seconds.

"What We Do Is Secret" only truly makes sense when you're a teenager. That's where The Germs excelled. They identify with their audience, maintaining a we're-all-in-this-together, they-hate-us-we-don't-care sense of community that would later inspire, fire and drive the US hardcore scene. It's what punk was originally all about – it gave the freaks a sense of belonging, something they could own and share. That's why punk was always about more than just the music.

**WHAT WE DO IS SECRET
COMPILATION ALBUM.
SLASH. 1981**

Guitar Wolf

Jet Generation

Sometimes the Japanese get hold of a western idea, have a go themselves and get it totally wrong – and the results are absolutely wonderful. Guitar Wolf are a classic example of this. If the sneering, spitting insolence of punk raised the hackles of respectable western society, imagine how much more shocking it must seem to a society like Japan, where politeness and deference to authority are almost art forms.

Described as "the freakin' three-headed love child of Godzilla and King Kong", "the coolest band ever in the history of rock'n'roll" and "the demon spawn of Joan Jett and Joey Ramone", Guitar Wolf are simply amazing. They've obviously aimed at a lean, mean, rock'n'roll sound pitched somewhere between the cartoon punk of The Ramones and the roaring junkie swagger of Johnny Thunders And The Heartbreakers. But they've ended up sounding like a plane crash. The noise they make is awesome. Screaming, primeval rock'n'roll heard amid screeching feedback and furiously screamed Jap-lish lyrics. It's raw and wild – it's the way you'd imagine punk would sound if you'd read all the hype but never actually heard any of the music. In short, Guitar Wolf sound like wolves with guitars. Or, rather, wolves with guitars making the kind of fucked-up, vicious, angry, snarling, carnivorous rock'n'roll that they would make if only they had fingers. (I love this band – can you tell?)

"Jet Generation" was originally conceived as a tribute to ultra-cool, leather-clad punk pioneer Joan Jett. It sounds absolutely nothing like her, but it somehow captures – ineptly but gloriously – the ultra-urban rebel chic that she sang about on her legendary punk pop hit "I Love Rock'n'Roll". Guitar Wolf are in agreement – they love rock'n'roll so much they fucked it.

JET GENERATION
ALBUM. MATADOR. 1999

Huggy Bear

Her Jazz

The grassroots 1990s neo-feminist punk Riot Grrl scene (inspired by Bikini Kill) was largely a US phenomenon, but it did produce one exceptional UK band – Huggy Bear – and one amazing single.

Riot Grrl – as interpreted by Huggy Bear – was a curious fusion of the old punk DIY (do-it-yourself) ethic and radical feminism. This led Huggy Bear to shun all interviews with the "sold out" music press and, in a couple of instances, physically to attack the male journalists who went to their shows. This, of course, did not make them very popular with male journalists.

In fact, men got beaten up quite regularly at Huggy Bear gigs, usually for pushing or otherwise harassing a female member of the audience, and the beating was usually administered by one of the female members of the band.

Huggy Bear were extreme but they had a point. Twenty-five years after punk bands like the Gang Of Four, The Mekons, the Au Pairs and Delta 5 had played Rock Against Sexism gigs, rock music (including allegedly "alternative" rock music) was still a male domain. Women who dared go down the front (even at what were supposed to be punk shows) were still getting jostled or groped. Or worse. And the music press still had a tendency to see women in bands as freaks. If Huggy Bear were extreme (and they were), then they were rebelling against an extremely shitty situation. Besides, since when has extremity been a bad thing in punk?

When "Her Jazz" was released in 1993, Huggy Bear were already causing a bit of a stir. They were invited to appear on the hip and happening British "zoo" TV show, *The Word*. And that's when the shit really hit the fan. The presenter attempted to interview a couple of huge-breasted *Playboy* models called the Barbie Twins. Huggy Bear and their fans, watching in the studio audience, stormed the stage, yelling that the show was sexist and accusing the presenter of "hating women". "You're fucking scared, you wanker!" yelled Chris from the band, as the presenter roared back, "Are you telling me I hate

Huggy Bear were notorious for eating male photographers.

my mother!?" A riot ensued, live on one of the most watched programmes on British television. It was hilarious and it was scary. And it was totally punk.

"Her Jazz" is musically and lyrically brilliant. It's a call to arms, not just through sloganeering (and Huggy bear were brilliant sloganeers) but also through a deranged, surreal argument between a female and a male singer. It sounds like The Slits trying to sound like X-Ray Spex but ending up sounding like Josie And The Pussycats having a nervous breakdown. And that, by the way, is high praise.

"Huggy Bear is a teddy sewn up full of dynamite."

**Fabian Ironside, Diary,
11 September 1994**

"Huggy Bear are an attention-seeking collection of spoiled brats who can't play music for toffee and who are milking the media for every scrap of publicity they can get. Revolution my arse."

**Letter to the British rock magazine,
*Melody Maker***

**HER JAZZ
SINGLE. CATCALL/WIIJA. 1993**

Husker Du
Divide And Conquer

"Makes No Sense At All" was the only single released from Husker Du's fifth full-length *Flip Your Wig*, but it's track 6, "Divide And Conquer", that stands out as classic mid-career Husker. With its exhilarating, eminently catchy riff and achingly poignant lyrics, "Divide And Conquer" bridged the divide between the ferocity of early '80s hardcore and the subsequent tidal wave of melodic and harmony-heavy '90s pop punk.

Reviewing *Flip Your Wig* in the *NME* during 1985, Richard Cook described "Divide And Conquer" as "about the lonely, hopeless citizen, the one who always locks his doors at night...the tracks sound like they're stretching up to something else."

Equipped with a lot more socio-political nous than many of their early '80s counterparts, Husker Du were also brilliant songwriters.

The term "divide and conquer" is a maxim used to describe a form of power management – popular with empires, dictatorships, racists and bosses of all kinds.

"Big brother on every wall/ Muzak plays in all the halls," barks Bob Mould gruffly over the top of a repetitive riff that's mind-numbingly hypnotic in its simplicity. Mould's lyrics are complex. On one level "Divide And Conquer" is a rant against the state's political machinery, especially in relation to the punk on the street, but it's also about modern America's culture of fear and paranoia – a theme that would be later explored in Michael Moore's brilliant movie *Bowling For Columbine*.

Husker Du maintained cult status throughout their careers. But considering the breathtaking (and more often than not abrasive) songwriting relationship of drummer Grant Hart and guitarist Bob Mould, it's criminal that they never scaled the heights of peers like REM – also a one-time underground indie rock act that went on to gain considerable mainstream notoriety.

The band's surreal third album – the acclaimed double *Zen Arcade* – was the nearest punk ever came to a concept album. The band split bitterly when the heroin-addicted Hart fell out with Mould following the suicide of band manager David Savoy. After a solo album, Hart formed Nova Mob. After two solo albums, Mould went on to enjoy further success and recognition with his power rock trio, Sugar.

Husker Du were kicked out of punk for this moustache.

FLIP YOUR WIG
ALBUM. SST. 1985

Iggy Pop And The Stooges
Raw Power

So why did punk happen when it did? The youth rebellion of the 1960s had finally ran out steam. The clothes and hairstyles that had once seemed so rebellious were now being worn by your mum and dad (and your teachers). And for some reason there were enough people who were both desperate for change and, crucially, were willing to *make* change happen. Then there were the Sex Pistols, a band simultaneously capable of outraging the mainstream media and of communicating their message of grass-roots rebellion to an eager audience of ordinary kids.

But punk– the music and the 'tude – had been invented long before that.

The big US chart hits in the summer of 1969 were "Aquarius" by The 5th Dimension, "Love Theme From A Summer Place" by Henry Mancini and "Sugar Sugar" by a bunch of cuddly cartoons called The Archies. The Stooges, fronted by a half-naked, gargoyle-faced streak of bone and gristle called Iggy Pop, were from Detroit, but they might as well have come from another planet.

Iggy And The Stooges sang about drugs, sex, death and destruction. Iggy slashed himself with broken beer bottles, smeared his reptilian body with peanut butter and dived into the audience. As with Johnny Rotten a few years later, the audience knew this was an act but found themselves simultaneously convinced that they were watching a genuine madman. The world wasn't ready for Iggy Pop.

At one 1972 London show, members of the audience panicked and ran for the exits. The young John Lydon – later to become Johnny Rotten of the Sex Pistols – was one of those who stayed and watched. And learned.

In 1972 the Stooges released their *Raw Power* album. The title track, with its droning guitars and hammered piano, was the sound of punk rock screaming to be born.

Iggy Pop seconds after kneeing himself in the balls.

> "Everybody's always tryin' to tell me what to do/ Don't you try, don 't you try to tell me what to do"

Iggy Pop

"We were a rip-snortin', super-heavy nitro-burnin', fuel-injected rock band that nobody in this world could touch..."

Iggy Pop

"The whole idea of punk...marked a process of deliberate unlearning; a new pop aesthetic that delighted in rock's essential barbarism."

Jon Savage, *England's Dreaming*

RAW POWER ALBUM. COLUMBIA. 1997 (THIS IS A RE-MIXED RE-ISSUE, VASTLY SUPERIOR TO THE 1972 ORIGINAL)

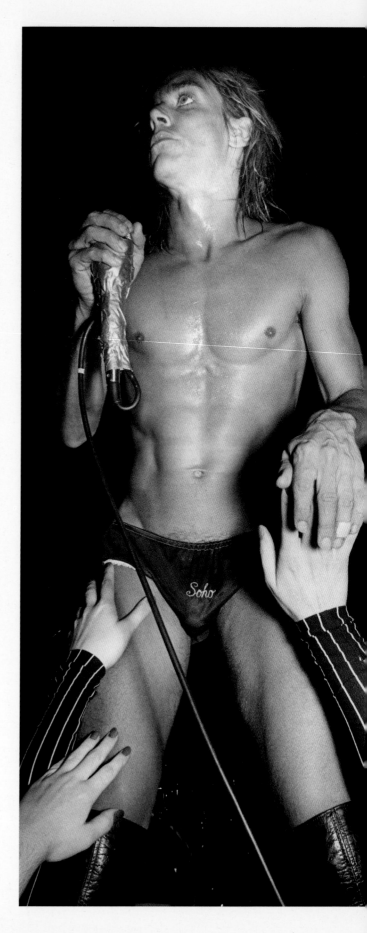

A female Iggy fan tries to get her knickers back.

Ikara Colt

Sink Venice

"Our music is one straight line with 'FUCK YOU' written on it."

Ikara Colt drummer Dominic Young

Ikara Colt burst onto a jaded London scene in the late 1990s wearing charity shop suits, sounding like a viciously speeded up version of the early Fall and Joy Division – and preaching the need for a new Year Zero for rock. Ikara Colt were of the opinion that, after five years, all bands should be taken out and shot, before they got the chance to get fat, old and smugly complacent.

Ikara Colt somehow distilled the tight, angular, aggressive, direct and political energy of the bands – like the Gang Of Four – who had taken punk in all sorts of interesting directions in the 1970s. The Colt turned that energy into something new, something fresh – and something that was desperately needed by a music scene that was awash with jingly-jangly "indie" bands.

The "speedy, volatile, spittle-dripping" Ikara Colt were described by one stunned critic as "slick mod-headed gunslingers who scream sex and hard drugs". Their live shows were amazing – the whole band twitched like Rialtin-addicted Tourettes-toddlers, seemingly always of the verge of pissing themselves with sheer fury. One critic claimed they contained all the energy of a Saturday night pub fight. Another confessed that Ikara Colt made him want to run outside and rip down "all the billboards and posters for any musician who doesn't have fiery vitriol coursing through their engorged veins".

"Sink Venice", the band's first single, is stripped-down, bleached-out, frantically minimalist art-punk. It is a ferocious, clattering musical manifesto made by angry youth in a terrific rush. Dominic Young slashes non-stop machine-gun vinegar-strokes out of his crumbling drum kit. Petite guitarist Claire Ingram and sweat-drenched bassist John Ball produce a skittering/droning wall of nervous noise. And frantically twitching Paul Resound sings – in a voice eerily reminiscent of both The Fall's Mark E Smith and Joy Division's Ian Curtis – about the need to destroy all the museums and art galleries (an obvious metaphor for the desperate need to do away with all the self-indulgent and tedious mock-rock that surrounds the band).

The result is a short, sharp and snarling distillation of Ikara Colt's speed-mod punk aesthetic. The song has its roots not only in 1970s punk but also in the artistic philosophy of futurism. This began way back in 1909 when the Italian poet Filippo Tommaso Marinetti wrote a "futurist manifesto" in celebration of the "machine-age". It was an amazing, proto-punk style condemnation of nostalgia and the obsession with the past, containing the line: "We will destroy the museums, libraries, academies of every kind…"

Although punk has always been about the new as opposed to the old, even back in 1977 some punk writers were talking about the "honourable past". By this they meant those artists and musicians who had previously stumbled across a punk-like need to tear down the rubbish that surrounded them and start again with something fresh and exciting. The UK punk scene, in particular, has regularly thrown up bands that are not afraid to admit they read books and that their philosophy has honourable intellectual antecedents.

The American writer Greil Marcus, after witnessing in slack-jawed awe a performance by the Sex Pistols, wrote that punk was about "denying the future that society had planned for you". Society has always expected its rock musicians to be stupid, uneducated and unwilling to learn. It is one of punk's continuing glories that it has always thrown up musicians willing and able to buck that demeaning stereotype.

Punk is not only still around but it also goes back a lot further than most people think. In fact, it is entirely possible that your great, great grandfather might have been a (really old-school) punk.

SINK VENICE
SINGLE. PLASTIC FANTASTIC.
2001

The Jam

Tube Station At Midnight

In the early 1980s the world media was awash with articles about "Tribal Britain". In the wake of punk, it seemed as if the island's entire young population had split into a bewildering kaleidoscope of competing youth cultures. There were peace-punks, anarcho-punks, peacock-punks and Oi-punks. There were goths, punk-goths, metal-heads, new wave of British heavy metal-heads, new romantics, futurists, 2-tone kids, rude boys, rude girls, rockabillys and psychobillys. There were left-wing redskins, right-wing nazi-skins, Oi-skins and even "skunks" (skin-punks). And some of the older youth cults of the 1950s and '60s seemed to be undergoing a revival, like the Teddy boys and the mods.

The mods had first emerged in the early 1960s. They were, as the writer Charles Shaar Murray put it, "as hard as painted nails". They dressed sharp (often in suits), danced to soul music, took speed, drove scooters and fought with their deadly rivals – the hairy, unwashed, long-haired, motorbike-riding "greasers".

The punk philosopher John Robb (singer with the punk bands The Membranes and Gold Blade) has put forward the theory that the slack, scruffy, laidback and peace-loving hippie is the "default mode" for youth, and that youth cultures that place an emphasis on speed, aggression and "sharpness" – like punk and mod – are refreshing attempts to break away from this lazy inertia.

Punk had far more in common with mod than it did with the hippies or the greasers, but one of the early UK punk bands took it a stage further. The Jam were mods. They wore the suits, they had the haircuts and they unashamedly looked back – not to The Ramones or Iggy Pop And The Stooges but to 1960s bands like The Kinks, the Small Faces and The Who. They played a speedy, guttural, short, sharp and aggressive music that sounded an awful lot like punk rock, but probably only because they weren't yet good enough at playing their instruments to come up with something more obviously mod-ish.

On their early single "All Around The World', singer Paul Weller spat out the line: "What's the point in saying destroy?" – an obvious put-down of the Sex Pistols. Weller would later go on to become a committed socialist but in 1977 he boasted he was going to vote for the right-wing Conservative Party. The Jam also placed themselves further outside the punk circus by performing in front of the British national flag – a symbol that, at the time, was associated in most people's minds with either the Queen's Silver Jubilee celebrations or with the neo-fascist National Front.

It was The Jam that Joe Strummer of The Clash had in mind when he wrote the lines: "They got Burton suits, ha you think it's funny/ Turning rebellion into money" in "(White Man) In Hammersmith Palais".

The Jam were not fascists. They definitely weren't royalists. They weren't even conservatives. But Paul Weller was a contrary bugger, eager to distance The Jam from the media hoo-ha that was increasingly surrounding punk. So, one way and another, The Jam stood out like sore thumbs from the rest of the punk bands. But they could not but help but be influenced and impassioned by the buzzing energy of the scene that was exploding all around them. More than that, in Paul Weller, The Jam possessed a songwriter of amazing talent, and it would be this talent – honed and polished to a diamond-hard and razor-sharp edge – that would enable The Jam to release a string of brilliant hit singles that would keep punk's flame alive even as most of their contemporaries crashed and burned all around them.

The lyrics of "Tube Station At Midnight" are a chilling narrative. They tell the story of an ordinary suburban office worker attacked by nazi skinheads in a London Underground railway station. It is an amazing lyric – one that would stand on its own as a poem, even without the haunting, panicked music.

Our nameless Joe Blow is alone and defenceless in the empty underground railway station. Figures intent on violence loom from the shadows.

The wolves descend on their prey.

The fists go in. The man crumples – and is kicked to death.

"I glanced back on my life, and thought about my wife/ 'Cause they took the keys – and she'll think it's me..."

The Jam's dress sense invited ridicule from Joe Strummer.

This was the downside of "Tribal Britain" – the horrific casual violence. "Tube Station" beautifully sums up Weller's bitter disillusion not only with youth culture but also with the city of London. This was the same Weller who once sang "the kids know where it's at", and who, as a suburban youth, had been so in love with Britain's capital city that he walked its streets with a tape recorder, just so he could relive the sound of its bustling energy when he got back home to the boring safety of his small-town home.

Never has disillusion been turned into such amazing music.

Eton Rifles

In class-conscious British society, a "chippy" person is someone from the working classes who is resentful of their social "betters". It stems back to the phrase "having a chip on your shoulder", which itself dates back to the days when a man seeking a fight in a pub would place a wooden chip on his shoulder and dare anybody else to try to knock it off.

Paul Weller has chips on both shoulders. "Eton Rifles" is The Jam's take on class warfare. It is an incredibly cynical and sarcastic song. The upper classes are portrayed as braying, arrogant thugs, made strong by rugby and accustomed to rule. The working classes, however, are weak, disorganized and slightly pathetic – no match for their brawny masters when it comes to fisticuffs: "All that rugby puts hairs on your chest/ What chance have you got against a tie and a crest?"

In the song's imagined gang fight between the classes, the workers get hammered and run off, leaving Weller alone, defenceless and embarrassed.

The "Eton" in the song title is a reference to Eton College, Britain's top private school and long a bastion of snobbery and unearned privilege. But it's the reference to rugby in the lyrics that's really interesting.

There are two sorts of rugby played in Britain. Rugby League is mostly played in northern England and is overwhelmingly a working-class game. Rugby Union is the southern English version and is notorious for attracting upper-class chaps who are both posh and very, very hard.

One of the reasons Britain had such a flourishing live music scene at the time of punk was that every college in the country had a heavily subsidized students union. The student union halls were often the only place kids in small towns could get to see new bands. Invariably, the braying "hoo-rays" (they'd be called "jocks" in the US) of the university Rugby Union club were chosen to do the security at punk shows. As often as not, the middle-class rugby players and the working-class punks would not hit it off – and would start hitting each other instead. The posh "rugger buggers" and the "chippy" punks were natural enemies.

In 1978, while on tour with The Jam, Paul Weller became involved in a nasty fracas with several rugby players in a hotel in Leeds. Weller came off worst. He suffered several broken bones and The Jam had to cancel their tour. Weller was also arrested by the police and charged with assault (although Leeds Crown Court would later acquit him).

This incident was undoubtedly in the back of Weller's mind when he wrote "Eton Rifles", but the song can be read on at least two other levels (he was a clever lad, was Paul). It can be seen as an attack on those punk "revolutionaries", like Joe Strummer of The Clash, who identified with the working classes while themselves

Paul Weller – the huge talent behind The Jam's string of hits.

coming from "posh" backgrounds. It was also about Weller's frustration with the very working class from which he himself came. When they got organized and fought back – as during the miner's strike of 1984 – they could be magnificent, but they also had a servile, cap-doffing, conservative streak. Most working-class Brits had fully supported Queen Elizabeth's Silver Jubilee (celebrating 25 years on the throne) in 1977 and had been appalled by the Sex Pistols' attempt to ruin it. In 1979, they would vote in their hundreds of thousands for the profoundly anti-working-class Conservative Party leader Margaret Thatcher (which was rightly described at the time as "like turkeys voting for Christmas").

Like the other Jam songs mentioned in this book, "Eton Rifles" is the work of a band pushing at the very limits of their not insignificant songwriting skills. The Jam at this stage were able to take a complicated and multi-layered song about class-consciousness straight into the mainstream pop charts. The Jam – the awkward punk outsiders – were well on the way to becoming the most successful of all the British punk bands.

Like "Eton Rifles", "Going Underground" also expresses Weller's growing horror at what was happening to Britain under the Thatcher government. The rich were getting richer and the poor were getting screwed. Schools and hospitals were being closed down to provide tax breaks for the wealthy. Entire industries (and with them entire working-class communities) were shut down for being "unprofitable". The army and the police were getting everything they asked for, while the health service had to hold charity raffles to buy essential equipment: "You'll see kidney machines replaced by rockets and guns."

Weller – the punk misfit who once claimed that he would vote for the Conservative Party – had became conservatism's most articulate and passionate critic. Here, if it is needed, is proof that The Jam were a punk band. The bigger they got, the more they shouted about injustice. British punk might have largely been tamed and co-opted by the mainstream, but that mainstream was now contaminated by left-wing bigmouths like Weller.

Going Underground

The single "Going Underground" crashed into the top position in the British charts in the first week of its release. This feat is even more amazing when one considers that it is an attack on the British public for being a bunch of blind, deaf and easily led consumerist sheep: "And the public gets what the public wants/ But I want nothing this society's got – I'm going underground."

There was a real irony here, and not only because what the public obviously wanted was more records by The Jam. Weller's declaration that he was going "underground" was ridiculous, coming as it did from a man who was probably the biggest pop star in Britain at the time.

The Jam had never been part of the punk DIY movement – the real underground – and by the time "Going Underground" reached Number 1 they were more than just another punk band. The Jam were pop stars. Huge pop stars. But this is to take the song at face value – and that's a daft thing to do with any of the brilliant, multi-layered lyrics that Weller was writing.

DOWN IN THE TUBE STATION AT MIDNIGHT / SO SAD ABOUT US / THE NIGHT
SINGLE. POLYDOR. 1978 (UK)

DOWN IN THE TUBE STATION AT MIDNIGHT / MR CLEAN
SINGLE. POLYDOR. 1978 (US)

ETON RIFLES /SHE SAW
SINGLE. POLYDOR. 1979

GOING UNDERGROUND / DREAMS OF CHILDREN
SINGLE. POLYDOR. 1980

Jilted John

Jilted John

"I believe in what Keats said about joy and melancholy, you know, all that is sad is beautiful and all that is beautiful is sad..."

Graham Fellows aka Jilted John

"He's a puff! And she's a slag! Yeah Yeah!" Jilted John – lyrical genius.

One of the great things about punk was hearing voices that sounded like yours and singing songs that reflected your life, not that of some out-of-touch millionaire who still thought he was "down with the kids".

"Jilted John" is a case in point. It was a punk novelty record. It was sung in the voice of a sad, pathetic, geeky little virgin who is all angry and upset because his girlfriend has gone off with another, bigger and cooler bloke called Gordon. She's "a slag", he whines, and Gordon's "a puff" (northern English playground slang for a male homosexual). It was beyond stupid. It was puerile. It was moronic. It was childish. But it was also funny and very, very true. And it was a huge hit in the UK.

The effect that punk had on comedy is often overlooked. In the wake of the Sex Pistols, the British stand-up comedy scene was revolutionized by a wave of furiously angry and extremely political "alternative" comedians. Four of these – Ben Elton, Rick Mayall, Ade Edmondson and Alexei Sayle – would go on to create the cult situation comedy *The Young Ones*, probably the punkiest mainstream TV programme ever.

Up in Newcastle a couple of young punks, inspired by the punk fanzines, put out a crudely photocopied DIY comic called *Viz*. It was crude, full of cock and fart jokes and low working-class humour. And it was very, very funny. But "Jilted John" was where punk comedy and punk music crossed over and crashed into the mainstream. It remains a very special moment.

Jilted John was the invention of a Manchester drama student called Graham Fellows. He's gone on to do other things since, but nothing that had the same impact as his sad and lonely little suburban punk. "Jilted John" might have lacked the dignity of other punk records but it told a truth. It told the story of what it's like to be the kind of guy who is ALWAYS going to get dumped in favour of guys like Gordon, and it remains an accurate and hilarious record of the way us spotty punk losers actually spoke back then. It is, in short, both a piece of throwaway novelty crap and a true punk classic.

BEST PUNK ALBUM IN THE WORLD...EVER!
JILTED JOHN. VIRGIN UK. 1995

Johnny Thunders And The Heartbreakers

Chinese Rocks

Those in the know were well aware that when they thrilled to Steve Jones's growling, grinding guitar work on the early Sex Pistols records, they were hearing the junkie-rock of New York's Heartbreakers stripped down and brutalized for a new generation.

Johnny Thunders And The Heartbreakers looked like the young Rolling Stones dragged through a hedge backwards. They took every drug they could get their hands on and they lived the legendary rock'n'roll lifestyle to its full (incredibly stupid) extremes. And they rocked like the mother of all bitches. They were too old-skool to be proper punk. They were too punky for the old-school rock fans. Shit, they were just one of the greatest balls-out, take-no-prisoners, fuck-you rock'n'roll bands of all time – and their influence on punk was massive.

The phrase "legendary guitarist" is way overused, but in the case of Johnny Thunders it is an accurate description. Thunders (and drummer Jerry Nolan) had been in a band called the New York Dolls. The Dolls played around with transvestism and sleazy glam-metal, and they'd been briefly managed by Malcolm McLaren (who would later put together and manage the Sex Pistols). At one stage McLaren even persuaded the band to dress up in red-leather jumpsuits adorned with the hammer and sickle – the symbol of international communism. Hardly surprisingly, this left American audiences agog. They weren't yet ready for such punky shenanigans.

When the Heartbreakers hit the UK in 1976 (to join the Sex Pistols, Clash and Damned on the ill-fated Anarchy tour), the press went mental. The exact same day that the Heartbreakers touched down at London's Heathrow airport, the Sex Pistols caused a nationwide scandal by swearing on a TV show. The British tabloids ate it up. Every front pages blazed with banner headlines about "the filth and the fury". Suddenly punk rock was big – and I mean BIG – news. And here were the originals. The band that had begat the Pistols. The New York Dolls – along with the MC5 and Iggy Pop And The Stooges – were one of the major influences on the British punk scene. "It was as if," babbled one excited onlooker, "the gods were walking among us."

Johnny Thunders and the Pistols were later to be involved in a musical feud. On their album *Never Mind The Bollocks*, the Sex Pistols bashed all things American on a track entitled "New York". Rightly or wrongly (probably rightly), Thunders took this personally and responded with the song "London Boys", which claimed that the English punks were so effete that they couldn't piss unless their mommies held their dicks. It was not, perhaps, punk rock's most dignified moment.

But while the Heartbreakers were a prime influence on punk and while their music was definitely punk rock played with balls the size of small planets, their subject matter harked back to an older and darker rock tradition.

"Chinese Rocks" is about heroin, the narcotic that has probably destroyed more musicians than any other, but the cool junkie rebel was still a powerful image in rock music in 1977. "Heroin chic" – wasted and whip thin – was the look to which most budding musicians still aspired. It was all bollocks, of course. Brilliant musicians who took heroin were brilliant (for a short while) despite the fact that they took heroin, not because of it.

Taken at face value, "Rocks" is an anti-drugs song. The plaster is falling off the wall, the girlfriend's gone,

> ## "It's like the kids who never did anything right, everyone they touch goes out of their minds – like someone who comes along and burns down your house."

Johnny Thunders explaining how he came up with the band's name

the guitar's in the pawn shop. "I could have been rich," whines the junkie in the song, but all he's really interested in is his next hit.

Like most "anti-drug" statements, its effectiveness is open to debate. I mean, if guys who took heroin could make music this ball-blisteringly fantastic, how bad could the stuff be? (The answer, kids, is very – HEROIN SUCKS.)

When it was released as a single in 1977, Charles Shaar Murray of the UK music paper *New Musical Express* was far from impressed: "Anyone who sings 'I'm living on a Chinese Rock' deserves to be marooned on one – you cool fool!"

OK, lecture over. "Chinese Rocks" (written by Dee Dee Ramone) rocks. All else is hot air and hoo-ha. Ironically enough, the song became the subject of a huge bidding war between two extremely well-known and family values-orientated soft-drinks corporations in the 1990s. Both wanted to use it in commercials for their colas. Can you spell "DUH"?

Born To Lose

An early Heartbreakers publicity campaign featured the band gushing blood over the caption: "Catch 'em while they're still alive." It might have been meant as a sick joke, but it was a joke that contained more than a grain of truth. The Heartbreakers didn't just dabble with danger – they courted it. They weren't the first band to do this and they wouldn't be the last. Sid Vicious, the Sex Pistols bass

Bloody brilliant – Johnny Thunders And The Heartbreakers.

player, would die alone and addicted to heroin – just another victim of the lifestyle that the Heartbreakers followed and glorified.

Rock bands don't turn kids into junkies, anymore than they make kids grab guns and decide to shoot up their high school, but the Heartbreakers aesthetic was already looking jaded by 1977. This was the year that rock was reborn. This was the year of hope and energy and activism. This was the year that the air positively seethed with possibilities. And it was also the year that the Heartbreakers released "Born To Lose". It was on the B-side of the "Chinese Rocks" single.

So the band that had been such a massive influence on the most positive rock'n'roll scene ever, celebrated its birth with one song about heroin addiction and another about the futility of hope.

And you know what? I couldn't give a toss. They are two of the greatest rock'n'roll songs ever recorded. End of story.

Well, almost. Johnny Thunders died of a heroin overdose in 1991.

L.A.M.F.
COMPILATION ALBUM.
JUNGLE. 2002

Jon The Postman

Toothache

The basic message of punk was that anybody could get up on stage and have a go. Jon The Postman was that anyone.

In his history of punk, *England's Dreaming*, Jon Savage writes: "Punk brought together suburban stylists, Bowie victims, teenage runaways, hardened '60s radicals, gay men and women, artists, disco dollies, criminals, drug addicts, prostitutes of all persuasions, football hooligans, intellectuals, big beat obsessives, outcasts from every class."

There's only one group missing from Jon's list – nutters, like Jon The Postman. But then Mr Savage is writing about ultra-cool London in 1976. Up in the north of England, in UK punk's second city of Manchester, things were even more mental. "You would see the Postman and his entourage of social misfits (fellow postmen, fanzine journalists, mad nurses, musicians, basketcases) at every happening gig," remembers the anonymous author of a Jon The Postman fansite.

Jon The Postman was a postman. Called Jon. He took drugs and he got drunk. He got on stage and screamed his way through whatever song came into his head. He had no discernible talent whatsoever but he didn't give a fuck. To many, Jon The Postman came to symbolize what punk was all about. Often, remembers the author of his fansite, shows would degenerate into drunken on-stage sexual orgies. "These were not beautiful people but people who looked like peeled potatoes and who would not normally inspire you to retain the contents of your stomach. This was not social or sexual liberation – it was just complete nonsense."

The Postman features in the movie *24-Hour Party People* – an hilarious history of the Manchester music scene from punk to the Happy Mondays. "There's one scene with Jon The Postman," remembers Manchester music scene big-wig Tony Wilson, "and the camera pans around the back of him and you see all these kids leaping up and down and fucking hanging and banging and beer flying out of their cans, and I thought – Fuck! This is exactly how it was in 1976 and 1977!"

Jon The Postman's Puerile came out on Bent Records in 1976. The sleeve was a brown paper bag. It featured a 25-minute version of "Louie Louie" with The Fall's Mark E Smith on vocals. One side played at 45 rpm, the other at 33 rpm. Even today, nobody is quite sure if it was a single, an EP or an album.

The opening track – "Toothache" – is an utterly incompetent attempt to re-create the sound of German experimental rockers Faust.

Musically there have been many better punk records. In fact, there have seldom been any worse. But that's to miss the point. Jon The Postman did it. He got on stage and he put out records. And everyone who ever saw him perform or listened to his music laughed like a drain. And then thought – "Fuck! If *he* can do it, so can I!"

Jon The Postman wasn't anybody special. He was just a postman called Jon. But in 1976 and 1977 he lived his life as if he were a superstar.

Jon The Postman WAS punk rock.

JON THE POSTMAN'S PUERILE EP. BENT RECORDS. 1976

Joy Division
Love Will Tear Us Apart

Joy Division were weird. While the rest of the UK drenched bands in spit and pogoed (the pogo was the first punk rock dance – you jumped up and down on the spot, as if on a pogo stick), audiences at Joy Division shows were notoriously static. Hailing from Manchester, Joy Division's greatest asset was their diagnosed epileptic singer Ian Curtis. Curtis spasmed as if electrocuted, his eyes rolled back in their hollow sockets, his gaunt face rigid with pain and angst.

The band also flirted with nazi imagery in a far more subtle and sinister way than those London and New York punks who adopted the swastika as a shock tactic. The band's name refers to the brothels that the SS maintained in its extermination camps. There was probably a very clever reason for this (one account has it that they took it from a book about concentration camps called *The House Of Dolls* by Karol Cetinsky), but at the time, when the modern-day nazis of the National Front were on the verge of becoming a serious electoral force in Britain, it struck a lot of people as incredibly dumb – especially when the band failed to explain themselves in interviews.

Joy Division were different. They sounded absolutely nothing like the Sex Pistols for a start. Instead they took the energy and urgency of punk and the bounce of disco and redirected it all into something altogether darker. They had a sound that was throbbingly intense – almost hypnotic. While The Buzzcocks – their Manchester contemporaries – were dissecting sex over irresistibly poppy buzzsaw guitars, Joy Division explored the dark side of the soul. The German philosopher Friedrich Nietzsche wrote: "Gaze long enough into the abyss and the abyss will gaze into you." Joy Division stared into that abyss long and hard. They were like the punk Munsters – only totally unfunny. Like I said, Joy Division were weird.

"Love Will Tear Us Apart" is undoubtedly Joy Division's finest moment. It is a hauntingly painful pop song. And most definitely a pop song – a million miles away from punk's early angry bluster. It's about pretty much the same thing as the Righteous Brothers karaoke classic "You've Lost That Loving Feelin'", but it tells the same story of love being lost with a far greater economy of words. The droning despair in Curtis's vocals cuts like a knife through the swirling, upbeat music. It is a classic.

On 18 May 1980, two days before Joy Division were due to leave for an American tour, Ian Curtis put on an Iggy Pop record and hanged himself.

His widow, Deborah, had the words "Love Will Tear Us Apart" carved on his tombstone.

LOVE WILL TEAR US APART / THESE DAYS
SINGLE. FACTORY. 1980

"The Che Guevara of punk" – Ian Curtis of Joy Division.

Kleenex

Heidi's Head

"The feeling of people breaking loose is irresistible: they sound like ten-year-olds maniacally cutting up their Barbie dolls...the band made a music where anything could happen."

Greil Marcus

In the UK punk was kept alive and invigorated by the John Peel show on BBC Radio 1. Peel – a former hippie who had learned his craft in the US – was a massive punk fan, but his show didn't just feature punk. He'd play absolutely anything – just as long as it was too mad, too rude, too stupid or too radical to be played on daytime radio. His impact on the UK punk scene cannot be underestimated. His love of the weird and wonderful dub reggae records coming out of Jamaica, and his willingness to play interesting music from all over the world – it all fed the UK punk rock melting pot.

It was on the John Peel show that the UK punks learned that there was a predominantly female punk band in, of all places, Switzerland. Switzerland! We knew punk was big in France, and we'd heard a few German bands, but Switzerland – the sterile and incredibly boring home of avalanches and strangulated yodelling. Switzerland – the country that was so obsessed with being clean and tidy that it was rumoured they actually polished their cows' hooves. This was proof that punk was becoming truly international.

And what's more it was real, cutting-edge stuff that sounded as fresh (if nor fresher) than anything coming out of London, Manchester or New York. We shouldn't really have been surprised. Kleenex's home town of Zurich was a hotbed of political activism, the local anarchists fighting regular street battles with the police, and the music these young hotheads heard coming from Britain made sense of their anger and frustration.

But the main reason Kleenex formed was "fun", says band member Marlene Marder. "I was listening to everything – blues, rock and roll. It started with the punk scene which came over from England. It's the old story. We were fed up with the old hippie bands and then the Sex Pistols came over and blah, blah, blah. We thought it was great fun and it was very easy to play."

"Heidi's Head" sounded nothing like the beefed- and speeded-up heavy metal that most fledgling punk bands were coming up with at the time. Instead it was a prime example of the way that bands like X-Ray Spex, Delta 5, the Au Pairs, Essential Logic, Devo, Prag Vec, The Slits and The Raincoats had just tossed rock's boring old rule book into the trash can and made something fresh, original and exciting instead.

"Heidi's Head" – made by non-musicians who still had their day jobs – is a classic example of the triumph of imagination and wit over mere technical skill. Critics would later accuse Kleenex – who had the hilarious ability to come up with lyrics like "Hotch-potch, hugger-mugger, bow-wow, hara-kiri, hoo-poo, huzza, hicc-up, humdrum, hexa-pod, hellcat, helter-skelter, hopscotch" – of being an "art band" and of reviving the European artistic tradition of Dadaism.

Dada had been an early 20th-century movement that had attempted to make art out of nonsense, daftness and gibberish. Kleenex denied any connection. They were just punking out. They were just having fun while wearing dresses made out of newspapers and making music that was as avant-garde as it was funny, political and catchy.

The band were forced to change their name (to Liliput) after legal pressure from the multinational corporation that manufactured Kleenex tissues. But the legacy of Kleenex/Liliput lingers on and can be clearly heard in the music of later American and British punk bands like Bikini Kill and Huggy Bear.

"They made radical social and aesthetic re-engineering sound like the greatest party you've ever been to in your life."

Sam Eccleston

AIN'T YOU / HEIDI'S HEAD
SINGLE. ROUGH TRADE. 1978

Magazine
Shot By Both Sides

Howard Devoto was an unlikely looking rock star. Balding from an early age, he was in the original line-up of The Buzzcocks and was largely responsible for the songs on that band's seminal *Spiral Scratch* EP. But The Buzzcocks wanted to be a pop-punk band and Devoto was into making music that was altogether heavier and darker. In his new group, Magazine, he got to make it.

"Shot By Both Sides" – Magazine's debut single – is a great song. Through swirling organs and over a thrilling, perpetually ascending guitar riff, Devoto creepily delivers lines that seem to have come from a film-noir inspired nightmare. He's "worming his way into the heart of the crowd" where a man asks him "why so twitchy, kid?"

Some gay punks interpreted the song as being about bisexuality. Gay politics were big news at the time and many gay kids had found in punk a place where their sexuality either didn't matter or was actually considered cool. After all, if everybody around you was dressed up as

a freak outsider and was attempting to shock "straight" society, who gave a damn if you fancied boys or girls?

Punk's flirtation with the gay scene reached its apotheosis when the Tom Robinson Band released their "Glad To Be Gay" single, which has got to be one of the punkiest pieces of music ever written. Punk troubadour Billy Bragg remembers coming to the huge Rock Against Racism concert in London's Victoria Park in 1978 and being stunned at the sight of a huge "Gays Against The Nazis" banner. Like most working-class kids in the 1970s, Billy's only concept of gayness came from the outrageously camp stereotypes in television sitcoms. Here, for the first time, he was meeting the real thing. And guess what – some of them were working-class punk kids just like him.

However, for all its talk of "liberation", there was also a strand of gay politics that was adamant that you had to choose. Gay or straight – which were you? And for bisexual kids – those who liked boys AND girls – that made no sense whatsoever,

As bisexual punker Laurence Brewer puts it: "As a young teenager the fun, rudeness, exhilaration and angst associated with the punk explosion gave me an outlet to express myself and my inspirations. 'Shot By Both Sides'…remind(s) me why I can be rude, irreverent and challenging to bigotry. This track represents for me the position bisexuals find themselves between straights and gays."

As tempting as this analysis might be (Buzzcocks singer Pete Shelley – who co-wrote the single's B-side – is/was openly bisexual), the truth is a little more mundane. Howard Devoto was merely saying that he thought that he'd probably be put up against a wall and shot by either a communist or fascist government.

SHOT BY BOTH SIDES /
MY MIND AIN'T SO OPEN
SINGLE. VIRGIN. 1978

The Mekons

Never Been In A Riot

It's 1977. I'm lining up to get into a Mekons gig. The student rugby player on the door takes exception to the way that some of the punks are dressed and refuses to let them in. Within minutes we've formed a "punk picket line" that nobody crosses. This is all tremendously exciting. After about 20 minutes the show's organizer comes running out to find out what's going on. We explain. He sacks the idiot on the door and, triumphantly, we march in to see The Mekons. Punk power!

The show is astounding. The band can barely play and after each song they all swap instruments. Then – in what now would be considered an act of madness – they stick the audience on the stage and play to us from the pit. Welcome to the weird and wonderful world of The Mekons.

Hailing from the same Leeds hotbed of anti-nazi and anti-sexist activism and bubbling punk energy as the Gang Of Four, The Mekons took the "anyone can do it" message of punk to its illogical extremes. For a start, anybody could be a Mekon – anybody who went to their shows was, by definition, considered to be in the band. For The Mekons, the division between the band and the crowd was non-existent. The audience were the show. This might seem like a ridiculous idea now, but in 1977 it was merely the truth. You'd regularly find yourself at gigs where everybody – and I mean everybody – was either in a band or selling a fanzine.

In their first music press interview, The Mekons all refused to give any second names – apart from "Mekon". And the only photo they'd allow to be published was a grainy shot of a row of suits hanging on a rack. This wasn't just the The Mekons being awkward. It was their attempt to put the anti-rock star stance of punk into practice. And, of course, it was terrific fun.

The Mekons were art students, well versed in such bizarre punk antecedents as Dada and surrealism. They weren't in a band just to make music. They were out to subvert just about everything, including the very idea of what "being in a band" meant. If they could get riotously drunk, batter a few fascists and have a great time

The Mekons – style gurus to a generation.

bashing out incredibly primitive but dead catchy pop punk at the same time, then all the better.

"Never Been In A Riot" – The Mekons' first single – came as a real shock to the punk system. For anybody who thought that to be in a punk band you had to be able to play your instruments as well as The Damned or the Sex Pistols, here was proof that you didn't actually need to be able to play your instruments at all!

The song, explains Tom Mekon, "was written about Terry's All-night Café – which was the only place in Leeds where you could get a cup of tea and a bacon sandwich at two in the morning. It was a real shit-hole. Almost Dickensian. And one night we were all sat in there and a load of police came in and ordered their bacon grill. Which we thought was funny at the time.

"But the song was also about this idea that was about at the time that you had to be street-fighter to be a punk. So it's written from the point of view of a bloke who's never actually been in a riot, never actually had a fight. And the closest he's ever got to it is when he's sat in this café and the police come in for some food. But the ironic thing, of course, was that we all had actually been in riots. You couldn't really avoid it at the time, what with the National Front marching and attacking our pubs.

"But one thing you have to mention," says Tom, "is that it was NOT a riposte to the The Clash's 'White Riot' like everybody seems to think."

"The Mekons are the most revolutionary group in the history of rock'n'roll."

Legendary US punk journalist Lester Bangs

WHERE WERE YOU / NEVER BEEN IN A RIOT SINGLE. FAST. 1978

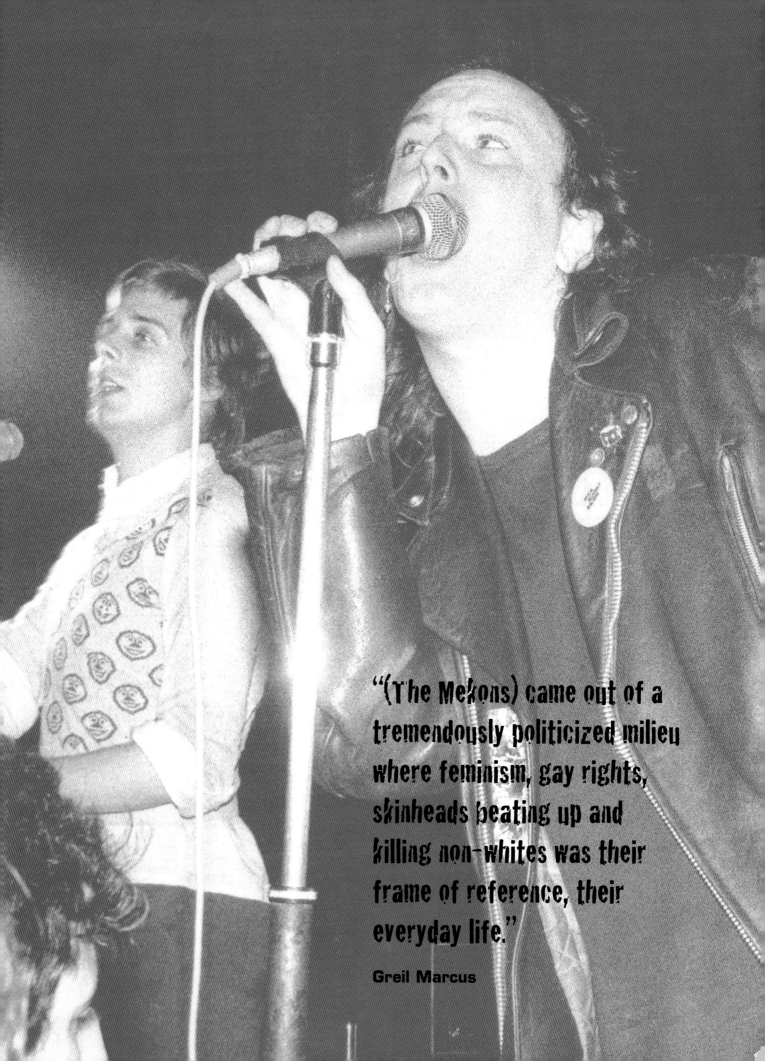

"(The Mekons) came out of a tremendously politicized milieu where feminism, gay rights, skinheads beating up and killing non-whites was their frame of reference, their everyday life."

Greil Marcus

The Members
Sound Of The Suburbs

Some of the best punk songs are actually about punk itself. These fall into three categories. There are those that mythologize it – like The Adverts' storming "One Chord Wonders". There are those that bemoan its decline – such as "(White Man) In Hammersmith Palais" by The Clash. And there are those, like "Sound Of The Suburbs", that celebrate the reality.

When US rock writer Lester Bangs visited the UK, he was amused to find just how nice and polite the English punks were. For all the tabloid press hysteria about punk, the truth is that most punkers were nice kids from nice homes where they lived with their nice parents (whom, of course, they drove insane by constantly playing punk rock records).

And that's what "Sound Of The Suburbs" is all about. Other records – the Pistols' "Anarchy In The UK" or The Clash's "White Riot" – might have articulated the energy and anger of punk, but The Members caught the reality of an entire generation of suburban high-school kids getting feverishly excited about punk in Britain's leafy and sedate suburbs.

Like "Jilted John" by Jilted John, "Sound Of The Suburbs" was a uniquely and delightfully English record – full of understatement and self-deprecating humour. It made great fun of the fact that most of these horrible, spitting, snarling punk rockers that everybody was reading about, were really just ordinary boys and girls having the time of their otherwise utterly boring lives, by dressing up daft and jumping around to mental-sounding music.

It's the "same old boring Sunday morning", moans singer Nicky Tesco over a throbbing, excited beat. Mum's in the kitchen cooking, dad's washing the car and "Johnny's upstairs in his bedroom sitting in the dark/ Annoying the neighbours with his punk rock electric guitar."

There then follows the shortest and most incredibly intense guitar solo in the history of rock. It is electrifying because you know EXACTLY what Tesco is singing about.

This is your story. This is the story of every kid who has ever dreamed of bursting out of the dull-as-ditchwater domesticity of their parental home to become a fucking rock star. This is PUNK ROCK!

"In those days lots of the fans were groups of kids from different neighbourhoods, they called themselves crews," remembers Members guitarist Jean-Marie Carroll.

"There was the Hampton Crew, the Fulham Crew and a group of nice Jewish boys called the Edgware Crew. We noticed that a lot of these kids came from the suburbs to see us. They were not hardcore inner-city types but fresh-faced kids who had heard the call of punk or 'new wave' and wanted some of it for themselves. Whilst a lot of our contemporaries were singing of inner-city problems, and having their photos taken in back alleys in leathers and sneers, we decided to go back to our roots to write a song about 'The Suburbs'.

"I actually wrote the early drafts sitting at my desk whilst working as a bank clerk. It is all about the area around Camberley, Surrey, where most of us grew up.

"In the second verse there's a reference to 'The Broadmoor Siren'. This is unique to the Camberley area. Broadmoor is a secure establishment for what might be termed the 'criminally insane' and they test the siren every Monday morning.

"The line – 'the bass is quite good/ the drums too loud/ but I can't hear the words' – refers to the fact that there is no sound of the suburbs. There is nothing there. It is a cultural wasteland. The same sentiment is echoed when Nick Tesco asks Johnny the punk what he's listening to out his bedroom window? The answer is that there is nothing there.

"This is the sound of the suburbs. The sound of Nothing!"

While it's true that punk attracted all kinds of freaks, weirdoes, neurotics, junkies, criminals, prostitutes and intellectuals, the greater (and largely unrecognized) truth is that punk was also a way for the normal, the straight and the boring to become something exotic and special. "Sound Of The Suburbs" manages both to celebrate that truth and to mock it at the same time. Its "slice-of-life" celebration of punk's pedestrian reality was a much needed antidote to the gloriously poetic hyperbole of the Pistols and The Clash.

When I first got into punk – sometime in early 1977 – I can remember being sneered at by the older kids who'd already been into the scene for, ooh, at least a year. By the time "Sound Of The Suburbs" came out, I can remember being appalled to learn that my little sister and her friends were calling themselves punk. I mean – they were just children!

When punk filtered down into the youth clubs and the playgrounds, the kids who lapped it up weren't readymade shake'n'bake ultra-tough devil-dogs. They were just kids. Clumsy, mumbling, spotty teenage nerds who grabbed at the chance punk gave them not only to be a part of something exciting, but also to reinvent themselves as anything they damn well wanted.

Not only is "Sound Of The Suburbs" a great punk record, it's also a damn funny and embarrassingly honest one as well.

The Members – nice boys from nice homes.

SOUND OF THE SUBURBS
SINGLE. VIRGIN. 1979

Thee Michelle Gun Elephant
Dead Star End

There are those who argue that, right at the moment, nobody does punk rock as well as the Japanese. I have to agree.

The band's unusual name is apparently a mispronunciation of the title of The Damned's 1979 album *Machine Gun Etiquette*, while the "thee" is a tribute to legendary British punk rocker Billy Childish (who has a band called Thee Headcoats).

TMGE play an "ultra-cool kung-fu garage punk" that combines punk with element of such pre-punk rock greats as The Who, Dr Feelgood and The Kinks. The results is a music that blisters the eardrums.

"Dead Star End" is pure Link Wray-style urban surf rock'n'roll with vocals that come straight from one of those sharp-suited and savagely violent Japanese gangster movies that Quentin Tarantino ripped off so brilliantly when he made *Reservoir Dogs*.

Ever since 1975 there have been those who claimed that punk is dead. Punk's demise was announced in 1976 and again in 1977. And just about every year since then some doomsayer has stepped forward to announce that the trip is now officially over.

But the truth is that wherever there are kids enthused by the idea of "just getting up and doing it", that's where you'll find punk rock.

**CASANOVA SNAKE
ALBUM. JUNGLE. 2001**

Minor Threat
Straight Edge

Straight-edge was a scene within the US hardcore scene. Straight-edge kids – disgusted with the alcohol and drug abuse of their parents and elder siblings – were punk monks. They didn't drink, they didn't do drugs and they didn't smoke. Many became vegans. Some of them went even further and swore off casual sex as well.

But forget any ideas you might have about straight-edge kids being wimps. Despite the lack of chemical stimulation (or maybe because of it), to enter "the pit" at a straight-edge show was to risk both life and limb. This was punk at its most brutal and physically aggressive. Some bands became fanatical about the straight-edge philosophy. I myself witnessed one straight-edge singer attack a smoking member of the audience with a baseball bat.

In some respects straight-edge was the logical conclusion of punk's need to distance itself from previous generations of rockers – to become the exact opposite of the stereotypical junkie rock star. The entire scene can be traced back to just one song – Minor Threat's "Straight Edge".

"I'm a person just like you, But I've got better things to do/ Than sit around and fuck my head, Hang out with the living dead."

Released on the band's self-titled debut EP in 1981, "Straight Edge" was a hurtling 45-second long rant against the idiocy of drink and drugs. It became the song that defined hardcore. It had everything – speed, brevity, attitude and furious indignation. Bad Brains apart, no other band has ever come close to surpassing Minor Threat's brilliant breakneck hardcore.

It is an amazing song. It runs at you full-tilt like a frothing pitbull, nothing else on its tiny mind other than clamping its jaw tightly around your throat. The first time you hear "Straight Edge", you feel like you've been assaulted and received a permanent scar for your trouble. "Fuck me, what the hell was that?!"

Minor Threat's Ian MacKaye shares the mic with a young Henry Rollins.

I said to a friend the first time he played me the track. "Put it on again…"

With a father who was a member of the White House staff, Minor Threat frontman Ian MacKaye had taken piano lessons from the age of three. Legend has it that some of Minor Threat's basic chord structures were hammered out on his mum's piano.

After deciding he didn't have the chops to cut it as a professional musician, MacKaye embraced the DIY amateur spirit of punk with his first band, the Teen Idles. One of the band's tracks, "I Drink Milk" (a song about the band's favourite beverage), could be considered as a precursor to "Straight Edge" (the song that thousands of punks worldwide would adopt as the mantra to a lifestyle choice).

MacKaye originally conceived the straight-edge philosophy as being about "controlling things and not letting them control you". This was somewhat ironic considering the almost religious bigotry of many who would later adopt the lifestyle.

In the US kids who were under the legal drinking age would have a cross drawn on the back of their hands as a warning to bar staff that they weren't allowed to be served alcohol. This cross soon became a badge of pride and the international symbol of straight-edge. Bands like the Teen Idles – who were all under 21 anyway – regularly played matinee gigs at all-ages venues that didn't have bars – keen to get away from the now inextricable link between seeing a band live and the presence of alcohol and/or drugs.

It was all about the music. A photo of a punk rocker with his forearms crossed and with marker pen crosses on his fisted hands features on the sleeve of the Teen Idles' *Minor Disturbance* EP (on Dischord Records, the punk label set up by Ian MacKaye and Teen Idle/Minor Threat drummer Jeff Nelson).

So was the entire straight-edge movement started because a bunch of underage punk kids tried to make a virtue out of the fact that they were too chicken to try to order a beer? It'd be funny to think so but, as far as MacKaye was concerned, abstinence was the ultimate form of punk rock rebellion.

In his youth Ian would go to see bands with his friend Henry Garfield (nowadays better known as ageing punk icon and TV presenter Henry Rollins) and goggle at so-called music fans who were zonked out of their head on Quaaludes when they could be witnessing Led Zeppelin live. Compared to that, living clean and staying in control looked like the much punkier option.

Predictably, straight-edge became the easy option for teenagers eager to assert their individuality by joining a fashionable crowd. In a short space of time, straight-edge became the opposite of what it was supposed to be. MacKaye had spawned a self-righteous monster.

The movement permeated many other sub-genres of punk in the '80s, the anarcho-punk scene especially. After all – ran the logic – how could you start a revolution if you're wasted on glue and cider? But, just like anarcho-punk, the straight-edge movement ended up as a parody of itself, a new generation of sheep-like followers seemingly unaware that it was supposed to about expressing one's individuality.

Tellingly, it wasn't uncommon for many in the straight-edge scene – like Youth Of Today's Ray Cappo – to take it to its illogical conclusion and become Hare Krishnas (a fate that befell more than a few of the original UK punks).

"Straight Edge" has been covered by every punk band and their dog, but perhaps the best version is NOFX's spoof (on their *White Trash, Two Heebs And A Bean* album) where the song is slowed down to a ridiculous jazz-waltz with "Wonderful World"/Louis Armstrong-style vocals. It is brilliant satire on the testosterone-fuelled jock world of 1990s hardcore.

With the Teen Idles and then Minor Threat, Ian MacKaye has for many years been hardcore punk's most fervent defender and best-known practitioner of the DIY ethic. Today he is still going strong with the band Fugazi.

MINOR THREAT
EP. DISCHORD. 1981

The Minutemen
This Ain't No Picnic

It's a sad fact that today The Minutemen are best known for the inclusion of their pseudo-polka tune "Corona" on the soundtrack of the *Jackass* movie.

With their keen political brains and a healthy fondness for satire and irony, the '70s Brit punk-influenced Minutemen have experimented with everything from freeform jazz to folk and hardcore punk.

Their legendary fourth album, 1984's *Double Nickels On The Dime*, saw The Minutemen at their peak. It's a 43-track mish-mash of diatribes and dialecticism and features the brilliant "Political Song For Michael Jackson To Sing" and the scathing "The Roar Of The Masses Could Be Farts".

The jazz-hardcore fusion of "This Ain't No Picnic" is typical of The Minutemen's refusal to dumbly follow the sound-alike hardcore punk template. The Minutemen were the most eclectic and avant-garde of all the '80s hardcore bands, and they stood out from the hundreds of generic, second-rate Black Flag wannabes that unfortunately came to dominate the scene.

"This Ain't No Picnic" tackles the subject of racism. It was inspired by a job one of the band had where his boss refused to let him tune in to any jazz or soul (or any other "nigger shit") on the radio. For that reason alone it is a stand-out track. Despite the fact that US hardcore was all but founded by the all-black Bad Brains, the scene was overwhelming composed of white kids, and for many of these kids America's rich and glorious history of black music was a closed book. This led to the generic, self-referential and monocultural sterility of much of hardcore punk. The Minutemen were a brilliant (but not unique) exception.

DOUBLE NICKELS ON THE DIME ALBUM. SST. 1984

Misfits
Mommy Can I Go Out And Kill Tonight

Named after Marilyn Monroe's final movie, the Misfits are more popular now than ever. The savagely funny song title is a perfect summation of the Misfits' ghoul-punk rock shock tactics but, while the original subject matter of the song lies in typical Misfits B-movie fantasy hokum, this explosive track has taken on something of a different meaning in a post-Columbine US education system. It's about the victims of the school bullies wreaking revenge on their tormentors.

This, of course, is a theme that has regularly been visited by punk songwriters (most spectacularly by the Boomtown Rats in "I Don't Like Mondays"). It's a logical extension of punk's affinity with the bullied and the downtrodden. Punk has always attracted the kind of kids who got picked on at school, and many would later take their revenge on the jocks and the snobs in their lyrics.

Harking back to the punk tradition of B-movie horror lyrics established by The Damned and The Adverts (see "Gary Gilmore's Eyes"), the Misfits paved the way for such modern shock-rockers (and defenders of the bullied) as Marilyn Manson, Slipknot and The Murderdolls.

"Singled out the kids who are mean to me/ Get straight A's but they still make fun"

COLLECTION COMPILATION ALBUM. PLAN 9. 1986

Mission Of Burma

Academy Fight Song

Formed in Boston in 1979, MOB mixed punk with pop and avant-garde experimentation. "Back then," recalls bassist Clint Conley, "if the music industry was a city or a village, we were definitely out in the bush staging raids with our little merry band of followers.

"Burma was sort of an acquired taste. We heard it over and over again throughout our career that people would see us the first time and it just wouldn't make any sense at all. Listening to our live tapes, I know what they're talking about. Sometimes it's just like chewing gravel or a visit to the dentist's office."

Once, Conley remembers, the band supported "the Dead Kennedys and Circle Jerks at some airplane hangar full of Huntington Beach skate punks. They were *outraged!*"

Burma were exploring similar territory to UK bands like the Gang Of Four, maintaining the punk energy but expanding its boundaries. And "Academy Fight Song" is Mission Of Burma at their brilliantly punkiest.

To this day Conley refuses to explain what the song is about. Is he telling a needy friend to fuck off? Or he making a more generalized statement about fascism? Aw, who cares? "Academy" is and will always be a stunning example of "avant-garde you can shake your fist to".

Mission Of Burma might have been tragically ignored when they were around, but they are now name-checked by everybody who knows anything about great music.

Mission Of Burma get the last laugh.

"Mission Of Burma played a noisily aggressive brand of guitar pop that was always real fuckin' close to just-what-the-doctor-ordered. But most of the time it seemed like nobody cared. Why? Well, people are assholes, I guess."

Byron Coley and Jimmy Johnson, *Forced Exposure*, 1985

ACADEMY FIGHT SONG
SINGLE. ACE OF HEARTS. 1980

Newtown Neurotics

Kick Out The Tories

After World War II the British government decided to alleviate the nation's chronic housing shortage (caused by German bombing) by building "new towns" in the countryside. These were heralded as a great social experiment, but unfortunately they were built without adequate social amenities – and without souls. The new towns soon became synonymous with boredom and squalor, so it wasn't all that surprising when the kids in these town took to punk big time.

Hailing from Harlow new town in the county of Essex, the Newtown Neurotics were never a big punk band but, in their anthem "Kick Out The Tories", they made one of punk's most passionately political records.

The Tories is another name for Britain's Conservative Party. Tory Leader Margaret Thatcher (imagine Ronald Reagan in a skirt) swept to power in 1979 and immediately declared war on the working class, on the poor, on immigrants and on other vulnerable minorities. For anybody on the political left (and most punks at the time were left-wingers), the next 18 years of Conservative rule were to be a nightmare.

"Kick Out The Tories" is a straightforward, no messing, scream from the punk heart. There is no attempt to be subtle here, to use poetic metaphor or to glamorize the class struggle. The Neurotics just want "the bastards" out and they want it NOW.

This is no bald Crass-style noise-fest. Unusually for the time (the single was released in 1982), the Neurotics eschewed the minimalist racket of anarcho-punk or hardcore and looked back instead to the "classic" punk sound of The Ramones.

"Kick Out The Tories" caught the mood of the country – or at least those that gave a damn. In 1984 the Tories constant attacks on the working class provoked the miners to go on strike (as fictionalized in the movie *Billy Elliot*). It was to prove to be one of the most bitter confrontations between British workers and their rulers in the nation's history. Many punk bands, including the Neurotics, rallied behind the miners, playing benefits and holding collections as the hated Tories tried to starve the miners back to work and used the police to try to beat them into submission.

"The general line is that rock'n'roll doesn't do anything, that it's politically redundant, it brings no change," said Steve Drewett at the time. "But I say, if we didn't do anything, we'd just go downhill right away. Our main worth, where I think we hit home the most, is not that we're making Thatcher shake in Number Ten [Downing Street], but hopefully we reach people's minds and give them something that makes them feel a bit more like carrying on.

"I'd like to take up a challenge. I'd like to see a proper, humane socialist government, and see the National Health Service back on its feet, and see a lot of things righted that are wrong. And then everyone can turn around to me and say, now what are you going to write about?"

"We want to see a caring socialist government in, the Tories out and to stop the rot within Britain and the western world as a whole. And we're going to do that with out next single, folks!"

Steve Drewett (with his tongue firmly in his cheek)

But the Tories would stay in power for another 12 years. In 1994 a punk band called S*M*A*S*H released their anti-Tory song "Kill Somebody" as a single (complete with a video that showed Margaret Thatcher's head on a stake and then-Conservative Prime Minister John Major being impaled by a guitar). S*M*A*S*H went much further than the Neurotics had done a decade earlier. They didn't just want the Tories removed from office. They wanted them executed.

When S*M*A*S*H played the song live, you could feel the electricity of sheer hatred sweep over the audience. You could see new punks and (now nearly middle-aged) 1977 punks almost weeping with emotion as they screamed the lyrics, their hands unconsciously curling into tightly clenched fists.

Two years later Britain's Conservative government finally fell. And they fell spectacularly. They lost the general election by the biggest margin ever seen in British political history. The rest of the country had finally, at long last, caught up with the Newtown Neurotics.

And Steve Drewett could at last get on with writing his love songs.

KICK OUT THE TORIES /
MINDLESS VIOLENCE
SINGLE. CNT. 1981

"Most of Harlow is people moved out of the East End [of London] – the true Cockney Rejects. But the communities they'd built up in the East End got destroyed in the move. My parents was telling me that when we first moved here, they'd go down any pub and there'd be terrific Cockney singsongs. That was when it was a really new newtown. Now it's dead. There is nothing."

Steve Drewett, singer/guitarist, Newtown Neurotics

Steve Drewett of the Newtown Neurotics gazes into the socialist future.

New York Dolls

Personality Crisis

In the early '70s the British pop charts were dominated by glam-rock. Glam was cheap and cheerful stomp-rock played by bands that, in the memorable words of one writer, "looked like bricklayers in drag".

Glam (imagine KISS with slightly less make-up and better tunes) would have a huge influence on punk (although, for obvious reasons, no one was going to admit this in 1977). And the missing link between glam-rock and the Sex Pistols is an American band called the New York Dolls.

The Dolls formed way back in 1971. They sounded like a cross between the Rolling Stones and T-Rex, and they looked like every mother's worst nightmare. They were incredibly loud and they sang about life in the gutter. And there are those who claim that they pretty much invented punk rock.

The New York Dolls were a mess. When the band toured England for the first time, the drummer promptly dropped dead from a drug overdose. Several of the band were heroin addicts and Dolls gigs were notorious for drug-related incidents – like band members falling off stage in a stoned stupor and then trying to inject themselves with heroin once they'd clambered back on stage. The New York Dolls were beyond dangerous – they were chaos incarnate.

By 1975 the group were on the slide and that's when they fell into the clutches of one Malcolm McLaren – a dodgy London boutique owner (with a genius for self-publicity) who would later go on to manage the Sex Pistols. Realizing that the band's transvestite-junky image was past its sell-by date, McLaren had the brilliant idea of getting them to dress in red leather and play in front of a huge, red communist flag. In America – the home of capitalism – these shock tactics had the effect of killing the band's career stone cold dead.

"Don't forget, the Vietnam War was still being fought," remembers Dolls guitarist Sylvain Sylvain. "We tried to be stoned-out, drag queen, transvestite freaks, or whatever. That didn't work. That's what they were

Communist transvestite junkie chic – the New York Dolls.

telling us – now you're gonna be fuckin' communists, you homosexual bastards! It was considered kamikaze. And it was. Typical New York Dolls, driving that freight train right into the wall."

The band would stagger on for a few years yet – much as a chicken runs around the yard when its head has been cut off. Guitarist Johnny Thunders left to form Johnny Thunders And The Heartbreakers. Malcolm McLaren flew back to London with his head buzzing with ideas. And the rest is punk rock history.

"Personality Crisis" is a prime slice of hollering, howling, stomping proto-punk sleaze. It's about the identity meltdown caused by drugs, but it's also about the maddening confusion felt by all teenagers – stoned or not. This would, of course, become a common theme for punk songwriters – most notably X-Ray Spex who covered the same ground (if less spectacularly) in "Identity".

The Dolls were a prime influence not only on the Sex Pistols but also on American bands like The Ramones and Richard Hell And The Voidoids. They started off trying to ape rock's previous generation, but they ended up helping to inspire the next. The New York Dolls are probably the most influential bunch of transvestite junkies in history.

NEW YORK DOLLS
ALBUM. MERCURY. 1973

999

Emergency

999 formed in 1977 and originally called themselves 48 Hours (after a song on the first Clash album). I have to admit here that 999 were nothing special. They made no great ideological, political or stylistic impact. They just had a couple of truly astounding songs. And this is one of them.

The name 999 is taken from the UK's emergency telephone number. Look, can I level with you? There is no story here. It's just a fucking great punk rock song. Honest.

EMERGENCY /
MY STREET STINKS
SINGLE. UNITED ARTISTS.
1978

The Nipple Erectors

King Of The Bop

In 1976 tombstone-toothed fanzine editor Shane MacGowan was a "face" on the London punk scene. Shane had won a scholarship to a top private school but had then been kicked out for possession of drugs. Along with many other misfits and ne'er-do-wells, he was to find his true home in the demented and often violent world of punk: "I mean, the punk thing fuckin' changed my life. It didn't matter that I was ugly. Know what I mean? Nothing mattered. It was good!"

At a Clash gig in 1976 a female punk smashed a beer bottle into the side of Shane's head. A photographer was on hand to capture the gruesomely bloody aftermath and the rumour soon sprang up that the girl had in fact bitten Shane's ear off.

Thus it was that Shane became a punk celebrity – one journalist called him "'the only original kamikaze punk" – and, one way or another, he's been one ever since.

Shane (by now named Shane O'Hooligan) formed a punk band with the incredibly stupid name The Nipple Erectors (later shortened to The Nips). Their first (and best) single was the deranged punk-rockabilly "King Of The Bop".

"King Of The Bop" sums up, perhaps better than any other punk song, the silly nonsensical and funny side of punk. "Why do they call me the king of the bop?" Shane asks, again and again. And again. "Because I am the king of the bop!" he answers. DUH!

The song is about Shane O'Hooligan himself – undisputed "king of the bop" at all the early Sex Pistols and Clash gigs. It was here that Shane amused/ annoyed the fuck out of everyone with his deranged, drugged-up and drunken "dancing". (There are even some who claim that he invented the classic punk dance, the pogo.)

Profound it was not, but it was extremely amusing. With "King Of The Bop", The Nipple Erectors can probably lay claim to the honour of having founded "psychobilly" (although The Cramps might possibly have something to say about that).

Shane of course would later go on to form the world-famous and massively successful Irish rock band, Pogue Mahone (later shortened to The Pogues). And he would become to alcoholism what Johnny Thunders is to heroin abuse.

"Pogue mahone", by the way, is Gaelic for "kiss my arse". Once a punk, always a punk...

"The way I see it is that we're coming up to the '80s and somebody's got to save rock'n'roll from all those prats with synthesizers and a university education. And it might as well be me!"

Shane MacGowan

KING OF THE BOP /
NERVOUS WRECK
SINGLE. SOHO. JUNE 1978

Shane tries his new dentures out on a tasty microphone.

Patti Smith
Rock'n'Roll Nigger

According to legendary groupie Cynthia Plastercaster, the 1960s groupie phenomenon really took off in the US thanks to the American girls who acted both as temporary girlfriends and surrogate mothers to visiting British rock musicians. It was as much about washing socks as it was sucking cocks. But it all turned nasty in the 1970s. Bands like Led Zeppelin delighted in humiliating and degrading their female fans. Out in the real world, women's liberation was putting the issue of equality right at the front of the political agenda, but in rock music – supposedly the most liberal of the liberal arts – male chauvinist piggery found a new lease of life.

Women have traditionally been marginalized in rock music. With a few noticeable exceptions, they have been kept in supporting roles – wife, groupie or girlfriend. Those female musicians who did appear – like glam-rocker Suzi Quatro or proto-punk band The Runaways – were easily dismissed as freakish novelties.

That would change – for a while – with punk. Although punk was still dominated by men, an amazing number of female musicians also emerged. Some – like Gaye Advert of The Adverts, Pauline Murray of Penetration and Siouxsie Sioux of Siouxsie And The Banshees – would become both icons and role models for future generations of female performers. Others – like the amazing Polly Styrene of X-Ray Spex – would totally undermine conventional notions of female sexuality. Still others – like the Au Pairs, Delta 5 and The Raincoats – would tackle sexism head on in their lyrics or through their support of the Rock Against Sexism campaign. And some – like Tina Weymouth of Talking Heads – would prove their worth simply by being brilliant musicians.

Punk didn't emerge all brand spanking new and wonderfully politically correct out of a social vacuum. It had its fair share of sexist meatheads but, for the first time in the history of rock music, it created a space where – for a while – women could make music in an

Patti Smith – punk incarnate.

atmosphere of equality. Perhaps this wouldn't have happened if the women in punk hadn't made it happen. Maybe it only occurred because the generation of long-haired rockers the punks were so intent on rebelling against were such a bunch of horribly sexist assholes. But happen it did.

And Patti Smith must take a lot of the credit for that. Before Patti Smith there were very few strong, wild, independent and musically brilliant female rock icons. After Patti Smith hundreds and then thousands of women decided – just like the punk boys – that they could be anything they damn well wanted to be.

Even in the current climate – where white rap fans habitually refer to each other as "nigger" – Patti Smith's "Rock'n'Roll Nigger" still has the power to shock. Echoing John Lennon's "Woman Is The Nigger Of The World", "Rock'n'Roll Nigger" is a powerful piece of rock'n'roll poetry.

"Jimi Hendrix was a nigger," sings Smith, "Jesus Christ and Grandma, too."

Like her fellow New York punk pioneer Richard Hell. Patti Smith was a poet as much as she was a rock'n'roller. Like Hell, she was often compared to the 19th-century French poet Arthur Rimbaud. Rimbaud was a revolutionary, a homosexual, a drunkard and an out-and-out social rebel. For the more intellectual end of the New York punk scene, Rimbaud was the original outsider, the first rock'n'roller and the prototype punk.

Like Richard Hell, Patti Smith was hooked on the idea of the artist as outsider – the "rock'n'roll nigger". In the 1970s African-Americans were only just starting to emerge from the shadow of slavery and the vicious and violent racist discrimination that followed in its wake. For over a hundred years, black American males had to watch their mouths. Any sign of being "uppity" could and did result in white violence and even murder. This is probably the origin of the very rock'n'roll concept of "cool". For white kids cool was a lifestyle choice. For black Americans it was a way of surviving while maintaining your dignity.

In the 20th century black America gave the world jazz, the blues and rock'n'roll. And with it came the concept of cool – of the hip outsider. The despised "nigger" became a role model for white kids seeking authenticity and rebellion.

Hardly surprisingly, Patti Smith received much criticism for writing "Rock'n'Roll Nigger". After all, it was pretty easy for a white woman to sing about being a "nigger", when the fact was that she didn't have to deal with the racism and prejudice that actually being black entailed. "I hate Patti Smith. She's a pretentious wretch," wrote rock critic Lester Bangs in *Phonograph Record* magazine.

He was right. "Rock'n'Roll Nigger" is an incredibly pretentious statement, but it is also ferocious and hypnotic. It is musical sheet-lightning, and the sheer boldness and brazen obnoxiousness of the lyrics make it one of the all-time great punk songs.

Patti Smith was a founding spirit of punk – every bit as much as Richard Hell or Iggy Pop – but without ever really being part of it. But here she is, back in 1975, screaming, growling or whispering her demented, furious incendiary poetry over the untuned howling of whichever punk guitarist happened to be around at the time. She's already establishing the first rule of punk (and the one that is most often forgotten) – punk is whatever YOU say it is. And I say it's Patti Smith, as much a part of punk's mythology as The Ramones or the Sex Pistols, but a far greater part of its soul because Patti Smith was wilder, more talented and, fuck it, punkier than any number of white boy guitar bands (complete with the requisite sneers and compulsory spiky haircuts). There are those that argue that Patti Smith has nothing to do with punk. Dude, she was punk.

I'll offer you the end of "Rock'n'Roll Nigger". Smith sings of her desire to be "outside of society" and then starts screaming the n-word until the speakers prolapse and the PC police run screaming from the building.

I rest my case.

"I want every faggot, grandmother, five-year-old and Chinaman to be able to hear my music and say YEAH!"

Patti Smith

Piss Factory

"Piss Factory" is one of those great punk records that definitely isn't punk rock (white guys shouting loudly over loud electric guitars). It's a poem about being 16 and having a shit job. And it is spoken over a tinkling piano. So what makes it punk?

"Piss Factory" was Smith's first single. I first heard it when I was 17 and doing a shit factory job. My head was full of punk rock buzz, I had dreams about starting a band, becoming a poet, putting out my own records. All around me were men and women who'd been doing the same shit job for years. They were dull-eyed and defeated. They laughed at my stupid punk naïvety. As far as they were concerned, this was real life. This was as good as it got. This was the future.

I knew what "Piss Factory" was about and so did tens of thousands of other kids who were turning to punk as a way out of a future filled with boredom and drudgery. "Piss Factory" is full of lines and images taken from rock'n'roll's past. It is a bitter, angry and frustrated poem. What the fuck is she doing here, stuck in the "piss factory"? When she could be Elvis, or soul legend Wilson Pickett?

It ends: "I'm gonna be so bad I'm gonna be a big star and I will never return...to burn out in this piss factory...Oh, watch me now."

We knew exactly what she was talking about. And, fuck yeah, it was punk.

HEY JOE / PISS FACTORY
SINGLE. MER. 1974 (RE-RELEASED BY SIRE IN 1977)

HORSES
ALBUM. ARISTA. 1975

RADIO ETHIOPIA
ALBUM. ARISTA. 1976

EASTER
ALBUM. ARISTA. 1978

Penetration

Don't Dictate

By 1976 punk bands were popping up in the unlikeliest of places. Huge fans of Patti Smith and enthused by having seen the Sex Pistols, a bunch of teenagers from an obscure northern English mining village called Ferryhill decided to have a go themselves. They named themselves after an Iggy Pop song, begged, scraped and borrowed enough cash to hire a van and set out for the bright lights of London. "I think we were a bit of a weird band really," remembers singer Pauline Murray. "We were always vulnerable. Looking back I think we were truer to what it was all about than anyone else. We were absolutely pure punk spirit."

The band travelled to London to play a gig at the now legendary Roxy Club (London's equivalent of New York's CBGB). There Pauline was disgusted to see how many of the London punks were wearing swastikas. "I hate fascism. I think it's shit," she spat.

Penetration were nice kids from respectable working-class families. Journalists who interviewed them were shocked to realize that they almost never swore. But the main focus of attention was Pauline – between Patti Smith and the arrival of Siouxsie Sioux (of Siouxsie And The Banshees), Pauline was a major icon and role model for female punks.

The music business would chew Penetration up and spit them out, as it would scores of naïve young punk bands, but Penetration did manage to release one amazing single. "Don't Dictate" rips off the chords from Black Sabbath's "Paranoid" but what makes it special is Pauline's beautiful, breathless and passionate singing.

"I was living at home at the time," says Pauline (in an interview for this book). "I was 17 and at that age you've had a lifetime with your parents saying – don't do this and don't do that – and I suppose it was time to say 'I'm going to do what I want to do'...The words are pretty self-explanatory. One of the verses repeats itself because we'd never written songs before and we couldn't think of a second verse. It was never one of our personal favourites...We kind of resented it really.

Penetration's Pauline Murray – punk icon.

"I think the song can be seen as a microcosm of the bigger issue. It's relevant in the wider sense as well. We came from a very small place, so it was also about the people who chased us down the street for looking different. We got a bit of that, I think a lot of punks did at the time. It probably goes on now, kids looking like Marilyn Manson getting their heads caved in at bus stops. That's the slightly bigger picture. And the even bigger picture is people's bigotry. I always took punk to be about self-expression, about being an individual. It wasn't just safety pins and spitting. All the bands sounded different, you know? So I suppose the song is about that too, in a way."

"Don't Dictate" was one of those punk songs – like "Oh Bondage Up Yours" by X-Ray Spex or "Liar" by The Clash – where (in the words of an old feminist slogan) the personal became the political. And it hit a real chord with the new and growing punk audience. After years of being told what to do, what to wear, what to listen to and how to behave, here was a scene that (to start off with at least) threw away the rule books. And in "Don't Dictate" it had found another anthem.

DON'T DICTATE / MONEY TALKS SINGLE. VIRGIN. NOVEMBER 1977

Plastic Bertrand
Ça Plane Pour Moi

It is entirely possible that Plastic Bertrand wasn't really a punk, and some people would claim that this means that "Ça Plane Pour Moi" isn't really a punk record, but those people can fuck off. Any record that sounds this punk rock is punk rock. End of story.

And what an utterly fantastic record it is. It's like sticking your head into a box full of wasps. It's a joyously fast, all guitars blasting piece of pure pop-punk nonsense, and I defy anybody with a brain and soul not to smile like a masturbating chimp every time they hear it.

Plastic Bertrand was the drummer in a Belgian band called Hubble Bubble. In 1978 he went solo, released "Ça Plane Pour Moi" and the world went crazy.

"Ça Plane Pour Moi" – a relentless, out-of-control, 90 mph-with-no-brakes imminent car crash of a song – was a huge worldwide hit. Undeniably as punky as hell, it reached people and places where punk had barely made an impact. It was just such a great pop record.

Meanwhile down in the punk clubs, there were those who would scowl and frown every time it was put on the turntable. This wasn't real punk. This wasn't proper punk. This wasn't authentic punk. But the younger punks just didn't give a fuck. They were too busy running around the room laughing like maniacs, which is what "Ça Plane Pour Moi" made you do – unless you were a wrinkled old purist with a stick up your arse.

Of course nobody who didn't speak French had a clue what the song was actually about. In fact, neither did the French speakers. The lyrics were totally insane: "A hangover drank my beer/ In large rubber glass/ Hou! Hou! Hou! Hou!" and so on.

Plastic fully embraced the crazy rock'n'roll lifestyle. He set fire to the curtains in a French hotel, and in New York he trashed his room with an axe and slung the debris out of the smashed window. What a star.

**ÇA PLANE POUR MOI
SINGLE. SIRE. 1978**

The Raincoats
Fairytale In The Supermarket

> "It was The Raincoats I related to most. They seemed like ordinary people playing extraordinary music."

Sonic Youth bassist Kim Gordon

In the sleeve notes for the 1992 Nirvana album *Incesticide*, grunge legend Kurt Cobain writes about coming to London and trying to track down a copy of the first Raincoats LP.

Eventually he finds ex-Raincoats guitarist Ana Da Silva working in an antiques shop. Da Silva promises to send him a copy.

"A few weeks later I received a vinyl copy of that wonderfully classic scripture with a personalized dust sleeve covered with xeroxed lyrics, pictures, and all the members' signatures. There was also a touching letter from Anna [sic]. It made me happier than playing in front of thousands of people each night, rock-god idolization from fans, music industry plankton kissing my ass, and the million dollars I made last year. It was one of the few really important things that I've been blessed with since becoming an untouchable boy genius."

Why, exactly, was the biggest rock star in the world spending so much time and energy trying to track down a long-deleted recording by an obscure all-female English punk band? Because the boy had taste, that's why. Kurt Cobain – the only true rock genius of his generation – was a punk rocker at heart. And he was also a massive punk fan. He knew his punk stuff, and he knew that The Raincoats were one of the most important punk bands ever.

Ex-Slits drummer Palmolive was the only Raincoat with any musical experience. Believing the punk propaganda that "anyone can do it", The Raincoats did just that – and made music that would inspire another generation of punk musicians in America. The Raincoats were the classic "can't play, will play" do-it-yourself punk band.

"I just felt so excited to see all these people dressed in different things," remembers Ana. "I went to a couple of gigs. People could just be something different from everybody else and nobody even bothered looking.

"Music had always been something that I was close to but it seemed to be made by people who were distant and, I felt, very much above me. With punk, both because of its nature and because I was living in the middle of it, music became something made by humans, not gods. Since we were also earthlings, we believed that we could have a go at it too.

"The punk scene gave us the opportunity to find our own voice…It took place in dingy little clubs with people wearing crazy things and doing crazy stuff. Of course it was full of prejudice and stupidity as well, but there was something very special about it. I would never in a million years have thought of starting a band in other circumstances.

"Punk, together with feminist ideas, made us women feel the world could also be ours, that we also have something to say, and that it should be said and thus maybe make a difference."

"Fairytale In The Supermarket" was The Raincoats' first single. Like The Mekons' "Never Been In A Riot", it is a brilliant example of the DIY punk ethic put into clattering, caterwauling and lyrically brilliant practice.

"It's all over now…Rock'n'roll is shit. It's dismal. Granddad danced to it. I'm not interested in it…I think music has reached an all-time low – except for The Raincoats."

John Lydon (formerly Johnny Rotten of the Sex Pistols), 1980

FAIRYTALE IN THE SUPERMARKET SINGLE. ROUGH TRADE. APRIL 1979

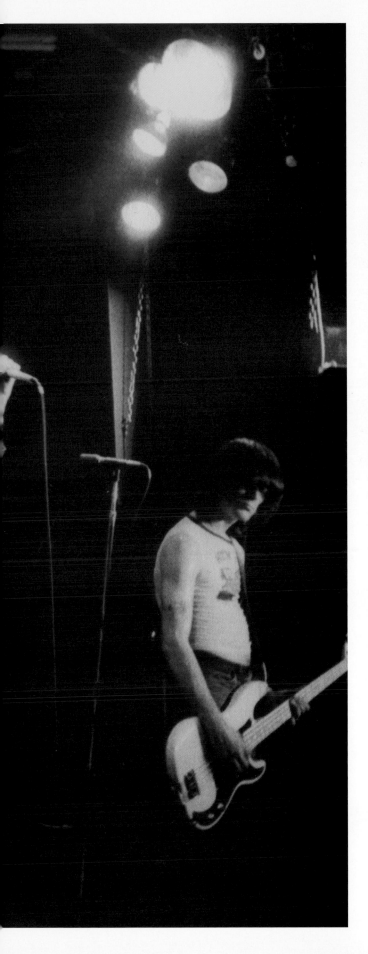

The Ramones

Sheena Is A Punk Rocker

"The Ramones are the latest bumptious band of degenerate no-talents whose most notable achievement to date is their ability to advance beyond the boundaries of New York City... The Ramones have absolutely nothing to say at all that is of relevance or importance and should be rightly filed and forgotten."

From a 1976 letter to the British *New Musical Express*, written by Steven Patrick Morrissey (who would later go on to be the singer in self-obsessed English "indie" band The Smiths)

Before the Sex Pistols there were The Ramones, who can truly claim to have "invented" punk rock. The Ramones made dumb, moronic, cartoon rock'n'roll. But in a good way, in a fantastic way, in an amazing way. The Ramones stripped rock music of all the pretentious "progressive" crap that it had become cluttered up with in the late 1960s and early 1970s. They stripped it down. They dumbed it up. They made it fun again.

America's answer to the Bay City Rollers – The Ramones.

The Ramones declared war on everything that mainstream 1970s rock music stood for. Before The Ramones, rock was bogged down in technically brilliant but sonically dull pseudo-intellectual bullshit (which is why The Ramones HAD to appear to be so dumb).

After The Ramones, every cool kid on the planet knew that the real truth lay in the short, sharp shock of buzzsaw-guitared, barbed-wire'n'bubble-gum pop punk. In the words of British punk/new-wave musician Elvis Costello: "If you can't say it in three minutes then why say it all?" Well, The Ramones agreed – only they usually said it in under two minutes.

The Ramones were the perfect rock'n'roll band. They had goofy grown-out Beatles haircuts and matching punk uniforms of shades, leather jackets, ultra-tight drainpipe jeans and baseball sneakers. These clothes were just like those worn by New York's "hustlers" – the male homosexual prostitutes whom respectable society considered the lowest of the low. Thanks to The Ramones, this look would soon become the costume of a million straight kids, and it still is today – just look at modern bands like The Strokes. And how fucking punk rock is that?

The Ramones were far from dumb but they sang about the dumbest shit imaginable. The Ramones were almost a concept band. They were a gang, but a gang composed entirely of geeky pinheads (who looked like an interstellar jet-lagged Martian's idea of cool rock'n'rollers). They were a joke band – but what a fantastic joke. Those who "got" The Ramones knew that they had to be incredibly clever to appear so stupendously stupid. Those who didn't get The Ramones probably never knew that the joke was on them all along.

The Ramones sang about sniffing glue and teenage lobotomies. While the biggest-selling rock stars of the day imagined themselves to be divinely inspired mystic geniuses, The Ramones presented themselves as mentally subnormal, socially dysfunctional, drug-wrecked total losers with single-figure IQs and the collective emotional maturity of a brain-damaged baby chimp – and they made it sound cool. Now that is genius.

More than any other punk band, The Ramones saved rock'n'roll from disappearing up its own pretentious hippie asshole. Their combination of Phil Spectoresque pop, 1960s surf guitars, blisteringly fast souped-up heavy metal aggression and total bang-up-to-date punk 'tude was irresistible. If you didn't like The Ramones – if you didn't *get* The Ramones – then, in cultural terms, you were already as good as dead.

"Sheena Is A Punk Rocker" was the hippie-filter *par excellence*. It was the record you played AT your long-haired, dope-smoking, prog-rock-loving hippie friends, and if it didn't make them want to cut their hair, throw away their flared trousers and make a bonfire out of their boring Yes, Genesis and Pink Floyd records, then nothing would. They were doomed to stay "boring old farts" forever.

"Sheena Is A Punk Rocker" is the perfect rock'n'roll record. What is it about? It's about a woman called Sheena. She's a punk rocker. Hey, what were you expecting? An expertly argued treatise on the influence of the concept of courtly love on 12th-century French Romantic poetry? Nah! Sheena *is* a punk rocker. The other kids are all going down "the discotheque au gogo" but not Sheena, because – you've guessed it – she's a punk rocker.

"To me, 'Sheena' was the first surf/punk rock/teenage rebellion song," said Joey Ramone. "I combined [the comic-book character] Sheena, Queen of the Jungle, with the primalness of punk rock. It was funny because all the girls in New York seemed to change their name to Sheena after that. Everybody was a Sheena."

Here is the all-time great founding punk statement. It asked which side you were on. It asked what you were intending to do with your stupid life. Were you going to spend your teenage years frightening the fuck out of the authorities by dressing up like your mum's worst nightmare, and going ape-shit crazy to the best rock'n'roll made since Elvis first swivelled his sexy young hips way back in the black'n'white '50s?

Or were you going to spend them in a dumb consumerist cattle-market disco, doing appalling John Travolta impersonations to the screeching horror-muzak of the The Bee Gees? Uh, gee! Let me think about that. For about half a nano-second.

"Sheena" is a perfect punk song, a perfect rock'n'roll song and a perfect pop song. It was pretty much laughed off the air in America but, astoundingly, it reached Number 22 in the British charts. The Ramones were John the Baptist to the Sex Pistols' Jesus Christ. They were heralds of a revolution.

Blitzkrieg Bop

Today the chant from "Blitzkrieg Bop" – The Ramones' first single – bellows out from the speakers at the start of every baseball game the New York Yankees play in their home stadium, and the tune has also been used in commercials for everything from beer to cell phones. But the song has an amazing – and controversial – history.

First, though, here's a bit of real history. In 1940 Nazi Germany invaded France, Belgium, Luxembourg and Holland. Using the revolutionary new tactic of combining fast-moving tank columns with air-support, they swept away the allied armies before them. This new tactic was known as *blitzkrieg* – German for "lightning war".

OK, fast forward now to 1975. A hideously ugly Scottish pop band called the Bay City Rollers have a hit record on both sides of the Atlantic with a catchy song called "Saturday Night". The Bay City Rollers were one of the first manufactured boy bands and as such are despised and hated by all fans of "proper" music.

Well, guess what? The Ramones were HUGE Bay City Rollers fans. "I hate to blow the mystique," said Joey Ramone, "but at the time we really liked bubblegum music, and we really liked the Bay City Rollers. Their song 'Saturday Night' had a great chant in it, so we wanted a song with a chant in it: 'Hey! Ho! Let's go!' 'Blitzkrieg Bop' was our 'Saturday Night'."

"Blitzkrieg Bop" is a celebration of teenage exhilaration. Nothing more, nothing less. But the use of the word "blitzkrieg" in the title and the inclusion of the line "shoot 'em in the back now" set alarm bells ringing.

This wouldn't be the last time The Ramones would be accused of using nazi imagery. The heavily (and obviously) ironic song "Today Your Love, Tomorrow The World" contained the lines "I'm a shock trooper in a stupor, Yes I am/ I'm a Nazi schatze, Y'know I fight for fatherland."

Looking back now, it is hard to imagine that anyone could fail to see that The Ramones had their tongues firmly in their cheeks. Especially when one learns that singer Joey Ramone was Jewish (and would later even be affectionately nicknamed "the Jewish grandmother of punk").

But that's to write with the advantage of hindsight. In 1975 and 1976 the New York punk scene was awash with unthinking, casual racism. The Dead Boys thought it was cool to scrawl "Hitler was right" on their guitar cases and the word "nigger" was tossed around the punk clubs and rehearsal rooms without a second thought.

Meanwhile, in London, many of the early UK punks were also using the swastika as shock tactic. It would take the arrival of the Rock Against Racism organization (and the publication of several timely anti-racist articles in the US and UK music press) before punk finally realized that racism (joking or otherwise) was a no-no, and for the scene to place itself firmly in the anti-racist camp.

In 1985 The Ramones wrote the song "Bonzo Goes To Bitburg". It was The Ramones' first and only political protest song, and it was written in disgust at US President Ronald Reagan's visit to a Nazi SS graveyard while on a trip to Europe.

OK, so that's that. Which leaves us with "Blitzkrieg Bop". All-time classic punk song. End of a very strange story.

RAMONES
ALBUM. SIRE. APRIL 1976

LEAVE HOME
ALBUM. SIRE. 1977

ROCKET TO RUSSIA
ALBUM. SIRE. 1977

IT'S ALIVE
LIVE ALBUM. SIRE. 1978
(ONE OF THE GREAT PUNK ALBUMS, AND ONE THE FINEST LIVE ALBUMS EVER – GET IT)

Rancid

Roots Radical

"I'm into Sick Of It All, Rancid, Offspring, all the new punk. I think it's a lot better than the old punk. The past gets cloying. It's got a dangerous magnetic pull-down. You get into vanity with collecting that old stuff like it's still 1977. I try to kick off traces of the past and say – let the new punk in!"

Joe Strummer, formerly of The Clash

San Francisco's Rancid are the classic example of the post-hardcore American punk band. They look back to the music of 1977, specifically the early Clash, for inspiration, but they turned those influences into something fresh and genuinely exciting. There are any number of old (and not so old) punks who rate their brilliant 1994 ...And Out Come The Wolves LP as one of the greatest punk albums of all time. And I have to agree. Rancid are as "4 real" as it gets.

"I'm a working class, dude," says Rancid guitarist Lars Frederiksen. "I know what it's like to work. My mom worked 13 hours a day and collected welfare to keep me and my brother alive. Never took anything for herself. It's like in punk rock: You listen to The Subhumans, to GBH, and you get all this information. Suddenly you're thinking – 'Fuck, I don't have to go to jail. I don't have

to kill old ladies. There's this, another possibility.' I think Rancid is putting that back. If I'm helping some kid in Bumfuck, Nebraska, and all he's got that he can relate to is that Rancid album, which is the way I was, that's what it's all about."

"Roots Radical" is a stand-out track on a stand-out album. Rancid take punk right back to the sound of west London in 1977. To the clanging hoot and holler of that glorious first Clash album. To a rock'n'roll that has one foot in punk and the other in Trenchtown, Jamaica. But Rancid have resurrected the spirit of '77 punk as much as the sound.

"People want to hear about themselves, real life," says Frederiksen. "People want to hear about things that affect them every day. They want to be able to identify and fit in, and I think there's a lot of alienation in the world today. Punk rock was one of those places where you could always go; I wasn't considered a freak because I was among freaks. It's okay to be fuckin' different."

Before he joined Rancid, gravel-voiced Tim Armstrong was a mess of drink and drugs. Other band members were forever driving him to detox centres or to hospital – and finally to a Salvation Army shelter. Tim had been there two weeks when another resident mistook him for a racist skinhead and threatened to kill him, and that's when Tim swore off the drugs and booze forever.

"I started Rancid right after," says Tim. "The rest was just having a dream. I needed something to believe in, to get me up in the morning and have hope for the future. Rancid filled that void.

"The time before Rancid was a horrible time. There isn't anything to look back on and romanticize...I checked into one detox ten times. When I was in there I had no fucking hope. I knew that in a couple of weeks I would be drunk again. It was a downward spiral. I didn't see any future. Maybe some people have that kick-ass, rock-and-roll, get-the-chicks experience with booze and drugs – mine was a horror show."

On "Roots Radical' the despair of the past – and a passionate (almost religious) fervour for punk rock – collide gloriously. The lyrics summon up a self-mythical punk rock San Francisco in much the same way that The Clash romanticized punk rock London. It is almost as if the two worlds, London in 1977 and California in

Tim Armstrong of Rancid.

the late 1980s, have collided, creating a world where the "punk rockers and the moonstompers" duck and dive and try to survive. And all the while a 1960s reggae soundtrack pumps away in the background.

But Tim Armstrong is looking through his rose-tinted x-ray spex with the drug-fucked eyes of his 15-year-old former self. "Roots Radical" is part bitter autobiography and part fist-clenched anthem. This is a song torn between nostalgia and cold-blooded reportage. Between hope and despair. And the result is beautiful, frightening and utterly exhilarating – all at the same time.

"Roots Radical" is The Clash's "(White Man) In Hammersmith Palais" for a new generation. But this isn't musical grave-robbing; this isn't a homage or a pastiche. This is the sound of the spirit of London 1977 reborn, refreshed and revitalized in modern-day California.

...AND OUT COME THE WOLVES ALBUM. EPITATH. 1995

"We're all like a pack of badgers. If you attack one of us, we'll regroup and attack you. We didn't grow up in nice neighbourhoods, we didn't go to college. We've got tattoos on our necks."

Lars Frederiksen

"Punk rock is my race, man. It's the colour of my skin."

Lars Frederiksen

Richard Hell And The Voidoids

(I Belong To The) Blank Generation

New York 1975. On stage are a band called Television. The singer, a spiky-haired youth in a ripped T-shirt and a biker's leather jacket, is having an on-stage row with the guitarist. The guitarist is Tom Verlaine and the singer is Richard Hell. Malcolm McLaren, manager of the New York Dolls and future manager of the Sex Pistols, is in the audience. Although nobody there knows it at the time, punk history is about to be made.

After the gig McLaren tries to recruit Hell for a band he's going to start in London but Hell refuses. "I just thought Richard Hell was incredible," McLaren told Sex Pistols' biographer Jon Savage in 1992.

"This look, this image of this guy, this spiky hair, everything about it – there was no question that I'd take it back to London. By being inspired by it, I was going to imitate it and transform it into something more English.

"I had these images that I came back with, it was like Marco Polo, or Walter Raleigh. These are the things I brought back: the image of this distressed, strange thing called Richard Hell. And this phrase, 'the blank generation.'"

Richard Hell left Television and joined Johnny Thunders And The Heartbreakers before forming his own band, Richard Hell And The Voidoids.

Hell, a former poet, didn't just come up with the punk image; he was also one of its founding philosophers. "One thing I wanted to bring back to rock'n'roll was the knowledge that you invent yourself…That's why I changed my name, why I did all the clothing style things, haircut, everything…That is the ultimate message of the New Wave: if you just amass the courage that is necessary, you can completely invent yourself. You can be your own hero, and once everybody is their own hero, then everybody is gonna be able to communicate with each other on a real basis rather than a hand-me-down set of societal standards."

The Voidoids' "Blank Generation" (which Hell had also sung with Television) was one of the first punk anthems. Hell had stumbled across the phrase "blank generation" in the back of a poetry book and was inspired to write a song along the lines of The Who's "My Generation". Most people assumed that Hell was saying that his own generation were "blank" – meaning that they were dumb and worthless – but most people were wrong.

Blankness, says Hell, "was kind of a defensive thing that kids that age will use. I think I felt just overwhelmed by input: the Vietnam War and the collapse of the '60s and the proliferation of media…it just felt like everything was too much to handle and you just tuned out. Blank seemed appropriate to me, because my own feeling was of sensory overload."

But the song had another meaning. "To me, 'blank' is a line where you can fill in anything," explained Hell. "It's positive. It's the idea that you have the option of making yourself anything you want, filling in the blank. And that's something that provides a uniquely powerful sense to this generation. It's saying – I entirely reject your standards for judging my behaviour!"

By 1977, of course, Richard Hell could only look on in amazement while Malcolm McLaren's bunch of English Hell-lookalikes started making press headlines. The Sex Pistols had arrived and kids in the UK were going mental over a tasty little number called "Pretty Vacant". Was it a rip off? I'll leave you to fill in the blanks…

Love Comes In Spurts

Despite his obnoxious on-stage image, Richard Hell remained a poet at heart. Like many punk pioneers, the noise he made was eclectic, experimental and adventurous – a million miles from the speeded-up heavy metal that later generations would think of as punk.

"I see how baffled fourth generation punks are when they first hear a Voidoids album," Hell told English rock writer Barney Hoskyns in 2002.

Richard Hell on a non-spiky day.

"They hear that this guy Richard Hell was THE original punk. But the Voidoids don't sound like the Sex Pistols, The Clash or The Ramones and that's punk to them. It's not just this barrage of stomping head-banging assault."

"Love Comes In Spurts" is pretty self-explanatory. For centuries romantic love had been the mainstay of poetry. For decades it had been the main subject matter of pop music. But here was the king punk himself, reducing all that beautiful poetry and uplifting pop down to a sneering line about the mechanics of male ejaculation. Nice!

The older, wiser (but still punky as fuck) Hell isn't so cynical these days. "Well, that was that kind of teenage wail of angst!" he told Barney Hoskyns. "It's not like it's my last word on romance!"

"We were much, much more interesting than the London scene that copped our styles."

Richard Hell

(I BELONG TO THE) BLANK GENERATION / (I COULD LIVE WITH YOU IN) ANOTHER WORLD / YOU GOTTA LOSE EP. ORK (STIFF IN THE UK). 1976

(I BELONG TO THE) BLANK GENERATION / LOVE COMES IN SPURTS SINGLE. SIRE. 1977

BLANK GENERATION ALBUM. SIRE. 1977

The Ruts
Babylon's Burning

In London in 1977 all the cool kids were into punk, but all the *really* cool kids were also into reggae. Reggae had evolved from its poppy ska roots into the militant soundtrack of Jamaica's struggle with poverty, gun crime and other third-world blights. It resonated on the streets of London, especially among the black youth being targeted by the city's notoriously racist police.

Ska had been popular with the (mostly white) skinheads of the early 1970s – in fact, the whole skinhead look was originally taken from the "rude-boy" image adopted by some young Jamaican immigrants. And many of the punks felt a similar affinity to reggae.

In some ways this was odd. The Rastafarians wore their hair long and smoked dope. The punks – at least in theory – despised dope and long hair, but the early example of The Clash (who enthused about reggae artists in their interviews) and a natural bond between two sets of exotically dressed rebels overcame such petty stylistic differences.

This is not to try to paint a picture of cosy racial harmony. Racism was rife in British society (it still is) and this was inevitably reflected in the punk scene, but in 1977 – after a couple of old rock stars had made public racist comments – concerned lefties with punk rock connections set up Rock Against Racism. It was massively successful. Large anti-racist carnivals took place in London and Manchester and scores of grassroots punk/reggae RAR clubs sprang up all over the country.

Many of the older "original" punks looked on this with something akin to disgust. They saw it as punk being hijacked by outsiders, but they were wrong. Rock Against Racism gave punk its soul. It turned what could have been just another cliquey, art-student dominated fad into the most politicized music scene ever.

The Ruts were one of the fruits of this newly righteous punk. They were a bunch of white boys from the multiracial Hayes/Southall area of London. They combined raw punk energy with the fluid loping rhythms of dub reggae in a way that was only ever (and only on occasion) matched by their musical heroes, The Clash.

The Ruts threw their support behind Rock Against Racism from day one. They also formed a fruitful and mutually inspiring relationship with a local reggae band called Misty In Roots (who were also RAR stalwarts).

They released a series of great singles (and one cracking, reggae- and jazz-tinged punk album) before lead singer Malcolm Owen died of a heroin overdose in 1980.

"Babylon's Burning" was their biggest-selling single. It's a short, sharp, two-and-a-half minute burst of apocalyptic fury, bursting with killer riffs, thundering basslines and Biblically intense lyrical imagery.

The song was originally called "London's Burning" – but The Clash beat them too it. "Babylon" is a term used by Rastafarians to describe modern western society. The Rastas, in turn, took it from the Bible, Babylon being the city the Jewish people were taken to as slaves.

For a group as lyrically and musically sophisticated as The Ruts, "Babylon's Burning' is an unusually raw and unsubtle hurricane of punk urgency. Ironically the song's chart success attracted large numbers of right-wing and National Front skinheads to Ruts shows. This was a problem that afflicted many punk bands of the time, particularly Sham 69 (whose singer, Jimmy Pursey, was more than once driven to tears by his moronic audience).

IN A RUT / H EYES
SINGLE. PEOPLE UNITE. 1979

BABYLON'S BURNING /
SOCIETY
SINGLE. VIRGIN. 1979

THE CRACK
ALBUM. VIRGIN. 1979

The Ruts' Malcolm Owen never did get the hang of shaving his eyebrows.

The Saints

This Perfect Day

In the mid-1970s Australia marketed itself as "the lucky country". It had beaches, it had sunshine and it had kangaroos. It was on another planet from the seductive sleaze and speed of New York or the grimy urban squalor of recession-hit London. Australia seemed like the last place on earth that punk would take root.

But it did. The Saints formed in Brisbane, united by a love of Iggy Pop and 1960s garage rock – and by a hatred of hippies. They were as much a gang as a band. They eagerly scoured the British and US music magazines and realized, with growing excitement, that they were not alone. There were others out there who had reached the same conclusions – that hair was to be worn short, that trousers were to be as tight as possible and that rock'n'roll needed to be rescued from the hippies who had ruined it.

The Saints were actually in the recording studio before any of the British punk bands (and before most of the Americans) but, as the punk focus shifted from New York to London, The Saints began to feel increasingly ignored and marginalized.

The Saints finally made it to England in May 1977. This was the start of the so-called Summer of Hate. But it was also the Summer of Hype. The sniffy London music press didn't treat the band too kindly. Richard Hell, The Clash and the Sex Pistols had firmly established the punk image – part male prostitute and part urban guerrilla – in the public mind. The Saints didn't fit the bill – guitarist Ed Keupper had grown his hair long in reaction to what he saw as punk's stifling uniformity. Despite the fact that only a year previously the music papers had been raving about the band's debut single, "I'm Stranded", this time round they were dismissed as second-rate Ramones copyists.

The horrible, shameful and tragic truth is The Saints weren't considered "cool" enough to be proper punk. Which was ridiculous – they'd been playing punk rock back when most of the Sex Pistols were still in school.

The proof is to be found in "This Perfect Day". It was the band's one and only UK chart hit and it's a title that instantly springs to the mind of anybody asked to list 1977's great punk songs (anybody who knows what they're talking about, anyway).

Jon Savage would later write in Mojo magazine: "'This Perfect Day' is the most ferocious 45 ever to grace the UK Top 40…"

He's not wrong.

THIS PERFECT DAY / L-I-E-S
SINGLE. EMI. 1977

"Rock music in the '70s was changed by three bands – the Sex Pistols, The Ramones and The Saints."

Bob Geldoff, singer with the Boomtown Rats and founder of Live Aid/Band Aid

"We were a punk group to start off with, we were a product of punk rock. The idea wouldn't have entered our heads if it hadn't been for seeing the Anarchy tour. In the early days, when Tom had just bought his kit and we had an acoustic guitar, we were very sort of punky in the old-fashioned way, which was fun. SMASH! DONG! WHADADADADA! Which is very funny to look back on, but we got tired of it very quickly. A lot of groups have managed to plod on and on for three years now. They must be bored to death with it by now. We got bored with it after three or four months."

Green, Scritti Politti singer, talking to Leroy Keene of *Printed Noise* fanzine, 1979

Scritti Politti
Skank Bloc Bologna

Scritti Politti are often described as "post-punk". This is a term used to pigeonhole those musicians who came out of punk but didn't play what is now thought of as "proper punk rock" (meaning macho speeded-up heavy metal with shouted lyrics).

This is just stupid, especially when one considers the fact that many of the "original" punk bands also made music that was brain-stretching (rather than just brain-battering). Thousands of bands erupted into existence in the years 1977–79, and a great many of them understood punk to mean that they should make music that sounded original and fresh rather than merely try to copy the Sex Pistols or The Damned. Scritti Politti were one such weird and wonderful band.

Scritti Politti were art students in the northern English city of Leeds (as were fellow punk revolutionaries The Mekons and Gang Of 4). Moving to London, they were inspired to put out their own records by the example of the DIY punk band the Desperate Bicycles.

The first Scritti Politti single, "Skank Bloc Bologna", duly hit the shops with sleeve notes that catalogued, in precise detail, exactly how much the record cost to make and how the band did it.

It was beautiful, strange music. It fused elements of dub-reggae to an almost gleefully technically incompetent punk buzz. The critics didn't know what to make of it but hundreds of kids did. They read the sleeve notes and went off to make DIY records of their own.

Scritti Politti were – like Gang Of Four – intellectual communists. In fact, singer Green had been badly beaten up for trying to set up a branch of the Young Communists in his native Wales when he was 15. But Scritti were less active than the Gang Of Four and less strident than the furiously socialist Clash. They were heavily into serious political theory and "Skank Bloc Bologna" was inspired by the writings of the Italian communist intellectual Antonio Gramsci.

Gramsci was one of the first writers to try to apply the rather rarefied economic theories of Karl Marx to everyday life. He is probably best known for his argument that "common sense" (the idea that things are the way they are because this is the way they are supposed to be) is a load of brainwashed bollocks. And that people's idea of what is "normal" or "natural" (and therefore "common sense") is often totally abnormal and completely unnatural and makes no fucking sense whatsoever (the dude was totally punk).

Like the Gang Of Four, Scritti Politti were actually covering pretty much the same sort of subject matter as less cerebral punk bands – like X-Ray Spex, for instance. They were just going into it in much more depth. All of which led to some incredibly complex and frankly rather boring music press interviews in which the band managed to make themselves look like pretentious bookworms.

Then again, given that punk was all about reinventing yourself, what was so wrong with pretension anyway? It was the "proper punk" bands (who were obsessed with the "common sense" ideals of "authenticity" and "keeping it real") who were the real bores.

SKANK BLOC BOLOGNA
SINGLE. ST PANCRAS. 1978

Scritti Politti brought a bit of pretension to punk.

Sex Pistols

Anarchy In The UK

Other bands (The Ramones and the New York Dolls) might have invented the punk sound. Richard Hell might have been the originator of the punk image. But the Sex Pistols came to define punk. They are THE punk band. They are the band that turned punk from a cool, cliquey, self-referential little rock'n'roll sub-genre into a worldwide musical, artistic and literary explosion. The Sex Pistols ripped punk off from New York and made it their own. They made it HAPPEN.

The Pistols added a uniquely British twist to the punk formula. They brought elements of pantomime (a strange and extremely camp British theatrical form where cross-dressed TV stars act out fairytales to audiences of baying children) to the punk party. They added a sneering, yobbish (and peculiarly English) social class hatred. They dressed like characters from the British kids comic *The Beano*. Guitarist Steve Jones wore a string vest and a knotted handkerchief on his head as a parody-cum-tribute to the great British tradition of looking like a drunken, scruffy bastard while on vacation. They were everything that was worst and best about the British – all wrapped into one explosive bundle of spitting hate and cynical fury.

They had in their camp some extremely clever art students – like record sleeve designer Jamie Reid (the guy who came up with the idea of sticking a safety pin through the Queen's nose on the cover of "God Save The Queen"). They had a couple of unreformed petty criminals in the band. They had an obnoxious bastard singer who looked like a crippled ginger ferret. And they ended up with a puny, violent and massively untalented bassist who would later murder his groupie girlfriend before dying of a heroin overdose (thus becoming an instant rock legend). But most of all they had – in the shape of the deeply unpleasant Malcolm McLaren – a manager with a ferocious appetite for causing as much trouble as possible.

The Sex Pistols story is well known (and anybody wanting to know more should check out Jon Savage's book *England's Dreaming*), but the bottom line is that before the Sex Pistols rock music was just the cool branch of showbiz. After the Sex Pistols, nothing would ever be the same again.

The first Sex Pistols single – "Anarchy In The UK" – is a solid blast of sonic energy. It is also very funny. Over Steve Jones's blasting guitar riffs, Johnny Rotten (in his trademark Cockney sneer) manages to rhyme "anarchist" with "anti-christ" and boasts about wanting to destroy (wait for it) "passers-by". What!? Sorry?

The humour of the Sex Pistols is often overlooked – and it's a very British sense of humour. One of the peculiar things about the citizens of that crowded island is that while they enjoy an international reputation for being frightfully polite, the reality is that they are actually the rudest people on the planet. The British sense of humour is based almost entirely on "taking the piss". On mockery and sarcasm. And the Sex Pistols were always taking the piss, not least out of themselves. They were the working-class cousins of *Monty Python's Flying Circus*.

The "anti-christ" is, of course, the form Satan takes on Earth in the Christian version of the apocalypse. Johnny Rotten, a skinny little London boy with bad teeth, was setting himself up as the ultimate evil, the prophet of doom and the bringer of chaos. He was, of course, taking the piss, and the fact that he was taken seriously – not least by the Christians who picketed Sex Pistols gigs and demanded that the band be forcibly stopped from corrupting the nation's youth with their filth and depravity – only made the joke funnier.

God Save The Queen

Britain is a constitutional monarchy. This means that the head of state holds office purely on the basis of the fact that she's descended from a bunch of inbred medieval cattle thieves. But the British are very attached to their Queen, and in 1977 they celebrated her Silver Jubilee (25 years on the throne) by holding flag-bedecked street parties and generally getting all patriotic and misty eyed.

Well, the Sex Pistols pissed on all that. "God Save The Queen" is also the title of the British national anthem, and its appropriation by the Sex Pistols was

Paul, Sid, Johnny and Steve – Monty Python's working-class cousins.

considered nothing less than blasphemous. Even worse, despite being blanket-banned by nearly every TV and radio station in the kingdom, it got to the Number 1 chart position in the very week that the Silver Jubilee celebrations reached their hysterical climax.

What a fucking amazing punk statement! Someone had left the Queen's cake out in the rain and the Sex Pistols had come along and shat on it. The BBC (Britain's "official" broadcasting organization) responded by pretending that the record was still stuck in the Number 2 position, but they weren't fooling anyone. The Sex Pistols – a pop group for God's sake – had publicly humiliated the British monarch and there was nothing anybody could do about it.

What's really clever about "God Save The Queen" is that it doesn't attack Her Majesty at all. Oh no, that would be far too obvious and easy. Instead it sympathizes with the old dear and instead turns its fire on the "fascist regime" that made her "a moron". "God Save The Queen" was about *everything*.

It was about growing up in a country where all the best jobs went to privately educated rich kids. It was about still being ruled by a bunch of horsefaced aristocratic scumbags with the IQs of cabbages. It was about being patronized and lied to and shat on. It was John Lennon's "Working Class" hero on speed and with a rocket from Russia up his scabby prole arse. It was about finally (at *fucking* last) hearing a band who felt as angry and as totally pissed off as you did (and were musically brilliant and dead clever into the bargain).

"We love our Queen!" sneered Rotten. Was he taking the piss? (Does the Pope shit in the woods?) The success of "God Save The Queen" was the perfect punk moment. Here was rock music as an event – as *the* event. Here was pop music that wasn't just entertainment – it was a statement. It wasn't just in the news – it was the news. This was the moment when everybody who had been watching the scene grow and change, suddenly realized that punk was something that was much, much more than just a fad or a fashion. Here was a music that made a real impact. That was

capable of making a real statement. And – best of all and most importantly – here was a music that really, really, REALLY pissed people off.

"God Save The Queen" was punk's D-Day. The lightbulb pinged. The penny dropped. The night sky filled with flaming fireworks. And the great thing was that we, the audience, weren't just going to watch the spectacle unfold. We were invited to take part. If we wanted to, we could become the spectacle.

The day that "God Save The Queen" got to Number 1 (fuck you, BBC) was the day the punk bomb exploded.

Pretty Vacant

"Pretty Vacant" is obviously inspired by Richard Hell's "Blank Generation" and it followed in the footsteps of The Ramones (who had built a career out of pretending to be morons).

This was a classic punk tactic. The tabloid press and the powers that be attack you for being stupid yobs, so you respond with a song that celebrates the fact that you *are* stupid yobs.

It was complete bollocks, of course. Yobs the Sex Pistols might have been, but they were one of the cleverest pop or rock bands ever. In fact, with "Pretty Vacant" they got away with shouting the word "cunt" throughout the song – and this time nobody at the BBC even noticed.

"Pretty Vacant" was the first song the Sex Pistols wrote, and was largely the work of bassist Glen Matlock (who would later be sacked and replaced with Sid Vicious). Glen was the quietest of the Sex Pistols. He was also, in the words of Johnny Rotten, "into the nice, clean-shaven side of pop". Rotten and Matlock would soon grow to hate each other.

The original idea for "Pretty Vacant" came from a Richard Hell And The Voidoids poster that manager Malcolm McLaren had brought back from New York. The song's lyrical hook "we're so pretty..." was taken from a newspaper article about teen pop sensations the Bay City Rollers. But it was about *us* – we were the scum of the earth. We were the new folk devils. We were your worst nightmare. And we were your children. BOO!

Holidays In The Sun

For centuries the image most foreigners held of the British was of the aloof, refined, frightfully polite but emotionally cold aristocrat. Then, in the 1960s and '70s, rising wages and the availability of cheap air travel meant that the British working class were for the first time able to take their vacations on the European mainland. Europe was in for a shock.

In the Sex Pistols' early days, they couldn't afford individual hotel rooms.

They discovered, to their horror, that the Brits were rude, loud, violent louts who drank like fish and cursed like troopers. This was a side of the British that the rest of the world hadn't seen before and it was a side that the Sex Pistols revelled in. Steve Jones delighted in dressing up like the stereotypical Brit on holiday, with string vest and a knotted hanky on his head.

Those who still couldn't afford foreign travel were catered for by "holiday camps". These institutions – the

two largest chains were Butlins and Pontins – offered cheap and cheerful food and cheap and cheerful entertainment – like knobbly-knees and glamorous grandmother competitions. In "Holidays" Rotten seems to be claiming that holiday resorts are the "new Belsen". Belsen was a Nazi concentration camp liberated by the British army in 1945.

Here, Rotten is quoting from the 1969 anarchist text *King Mob Echo*: "Monopoly capitalism will construct its own ministry of leisure over western Europe: Butlins camps or rarefied Belsens all along the Costa Brava."

The single's sleeve was designed by Jamie Reid (who did all of the Sex Pistols' amazing artwork). This led to a lawsuit from the Belgian Travel Service, whose brochure Reid had shamelessly ripped off.

For any other band this might have been a calamity but for the Pistols it was just another day at the office. Manager Malcolm McLaren actively sought such controversy and barely a day passed without some shock-horror Sex Pistols story hitting the tabloids (including the incident where Johnny Rotten was beaten up by indignant royalist Teddy boys).

For the tough Steve Jones this was all water off a punk-duck's back, but for the thoughtful and surprisingly sensitive Rotten, the pressure of being public enemy number one was getting to be too much. "Holidays In The Sun" is the sound of punk teetering on the brink of a nervous breakdown.

"Holidays" starts with the sound of jackboots crunching on gravel and goes on to mention the Berlin Wall (built by the communist East German government to stop people from escaping to the west). It then turns into an hysterical attack on consumerism and capitalism and the notion of having "a cheap holiday in somebody else's misery". Like most Sex Pistols songs, "Holidays" is about everything and it is about nothing. Musically it is a macho heavy metal stomp. Lyrically it is a neurotic mess. And it is the Sex Pistols' masterpiece.

"Holidays In The Sun" is built around a riff that Jones (a self-confessed thief before and after he joined the Sex Pistols) brazenly stole from The Jam's "In The City".

This would later lead to a confrontation between the Pistols' weedy bassist, Sid Vicious, and The Jam's Paul Weller (in which Sid got his scrawny ass kicked). The nightmarish lyrics were inspired by a trip the Sex Pistols made to the British holiday island of Jersey (they hated it – natch) before flying on to the divided city of Berlin.

Berlin was on the frontline of the cold war between the capitalist west and the communist east. In "Holidays" Rotten pleads hysterically for someone (himself?) not to be made to go over the wall, but eventually he takes a peek. And guess what? "I'm looking over the wall/ AND THEY'RE LOOKING AT ME!"

It's as if Rotten has just woken up from a fevered and sweat-soaked nightmare and is now recounting the insane and incoherent details. "Holidays" reeks of paranoia and pain. Little did we know it but it was also an accurate account of Rotten's state of mind at the time. The Sex Pistols had burned so brightly that they were now almost burned out. The end was nigh. But what a way to go.

ANARCHY IN THE UK /
I WANNA BE ME
SINGLE. EMI. NOVEMBER 1976

GOD SAVE THE QUEEN /
DID YOU NO WRONG
SINGLE. VIRGIN. MAY 1977

PRETTY VACANT / NO FUN
SINGLE. VIRGIN. JULY 1977

HOLIDAYS IN THE SUN /
SATELLITE
SINGLE. VIRGIN. OCTOBER 1977

NEVER MIND THE BOLLOCKS
HERE'S THE SEX PISTOLS
ALBUM. VIRGIN. 1977

Sham 69

If The Kids Are United

"Sham 69 play rock'n'roll in the manner that American negroes fight, not for fun but for existence."

Punk journalist Julie Burchill, *New Musical Express*, 1977

Sham 69 were a Bay City Rollers tribute band before they discovered punk. They had in Jimmy Pursey a singer who, in the cruel words of punk journalist Julie Burchill, was "living proof that one requires a modicum of intelligence to be a spokesman for one's generation".

This was funny but unfair. Pursey never claimed to be an intellectual. He just told it the way he – an ordinary suburban working-class kid – saw it, and he hit a chord with thousands of kids who felt the same way. Sham specialized in street punk (later to be called Oi) – fast

Angels with dirty faces – Sham 69.

and furious and with soccer hooligan-style chant-along choruses. Unfortunately this brought them to the attention of the revitalized skinhead movement, a number of whom were supporters of the far-right National Front.

Pursey was a committed anti-fascist and Sham had played the big Rock Against Racism carnival in London in 1978. He despaired of this new neo-nazi following (and of their distressing habit of turning every Sham shown into a mass brawl).

"Kids" was Jimmy's attempt to put things right. It was a call for youth unity – black and white, punk and skinhead. Jimmy pleads with the listener to realize that the punk/mod/skin stood next to them was "a kid with feelings like you and me". He promised that "if the kids are united they will never be divided". This was based on a socialist chant – "The workers united will never be defeated" – that was often heard on British streets in the strike-torn 1970s.

So did it work? Did the kids unite, never again to be divided? And did this stop all the fighting at Sham gigs? The acid test came when Sham were invited to play Britain's Reading Festival. Reading had always been a bit of a hippie gig and the inclusion of Sham and several other punk bands was generally regarded as a breakthrough. So where better for Jimmy to showcase his new, inclusive, empowering and ghetto-busting anthem of peace and unity?

To start with, it all went well. Jimmy had invited long-haired hippie Steve Hillage to play guitar on "Kids". Several skinheads jumped on the stage but they seemed more intent on having a dance than on causing trouble. So it was hippies and punks and skins altogether in a show of unity – just as Jimmy intended.

And then, just as the last power chord faded away, a big fat skinhead wearing a National Front T-shirt grabbed the microphone and bellowed: "And if you don't like it, hippies, you can FUCK OFF!"

Sadly, that one incident pretty much summed up Sham 69's entire career.

**IF THE KIDS ARE UNITED / SUNDAY MORNING NIGHTMARE
SINGLE. POLYDOR. 1978**

Shampoo

Trouble

You think the Spice Girls invented "girl power"? Meet Shampoo. And be afraid. Be very afraid. Shampoo were fans of the Manic Street Preachers. They were blonde and cute – in the way that rabid wolf puppies are cute. Often mistaken for twins, they were notoriously uncommunicative and generally reacted to the outside world with a sneering giggle.

And so, naturally enough, somebody decided that they ought to be pop stars. The fact that they were very average singers with no proven songwriting ability was not seen as a disadvantage.

Looking like Barbie dolls with the eyes of hungry Alsatian dogs, Shampoo explored the trashier end of punk. While all around them were getting terribly excited about the punk feminism of bands like Huggy Bear and Bikini Kill, Shampoo were coming up with lyrics like: "Hippie chicks are sad and super models suck/ Riot grrls, diet girls – who really gives a fuck?" ("Viva La Megababes").

Shampoo thought pop was shit. They thought rock was shit. They thought old men banging on about how Shampoo were punk were shit. They thought I was shit. And, had they ever met you, they would probably have thought that you were shit, too. Shampoo were the spiritual granddaughters of Sid Vicious and Debbie Harry. I shit you not.

"I wanna play with knives, I wanna play with guns/ I wanna smash the place up just for fun…" ("Girl Power").

"Trouble" was probably the best pop-punk single since Plastic Bertrand's epic "Ça Plane Pour Moi". Part soccer terrace anthem and part psychotic bubblegum pop, our two dead-eyed minxes sing about being late home from a night out and the trouble this is going to get them into:

"The party was great, yeah, we were really frilled [sic]/ and when we get home we're gonna get killed!"

Despite being massive in Japan (where they are still worshipped as punk goddesses), Shampoo never achieved the success they deserved in the UK and the US. Then the Spice Girls came along and glammed up (and de-punked) girl power for the masses. BOO! HISS!

**TROUBLE
SINGLE. FOOD. 1995**

Siouxsie And The Banshees
Hong Kong Garden

Siouxsie And The Banshees were one of the last bands to emerge from the original London punk scene that had spat forth the likes of X-Ray Spex, the Sex Pistols and Generation X. And they were also one of the best.

The Banshees first formed in 1976 as a hastily scrambled together support band for the Sex Pistols. With Sid Vicious (later to join the Pistols) on drums, the performance was a (now fondly remembered) total disaster with the under-rehearsed and utterly incompetent "musicians" stumbling their way through everything from a 20-minute version of the Lord's Prayer to covers of Bay City Rollers songs.

Siouxsie later told Sex Pistols' biographer Jon Savage that the band had chosen their eccentric set list on the basis of: "What song do you hate? What would you like to throw in as a shock tactic? What can we mutilate and destroy?"

The Banshees then disappeared, but when they re-emerged (minus Sid) they sounded astounding. They played a music that was harsher, more angular and more discordant than most of their peers. They were a joyless bunch, the Banshees, deadly serious and always keeping a cool distance between themselves and punk's more laddish tendencies. The Banshees co-opted elements of the 1930s Bauhaus art movement and the work of anti-nazi montage artist John Heartfield into their imagery and music. They were not mucking around.

The band's focal point was Siouxsie Sioux, a black-clad, heavily made up punk diva with a shock of black hair. Siouxsie would become the female punk role model *par excellence*. In fact, she pretty much invented the female goth look (although the Banshees were never a goth band). She had been an early Sex Pistols fan, part of the now legendary Bromley Contingent (which also featured Billy Idol among its number).

"Hong Kong Garden" is a song with an anti-racist message – which is kind of ironic given that, at the Banshees' now-legendary first show, Clash manager Bernie Rhodes refused to lend the band The Clash's PA because he objected to Siouxsie's swastika armband.

Siouxsie wrote the lyrics about the racism suffered by the staff in her local Chinese restaurant, but this message is conveyed in a series of racially stereotyped comments about Chinese food and "slanted eyes". The Banshees relied on their audience to spot the irony (which is never a wise thing to do).

Punk was already splintering into a dozen different sub-genres in the summer of 1978. The punk audience were itching for a change and "Hong Kong Garden" came along just at the right time. Musically it was astounding – a million miles from the crash, bash thud chaos of their first appearance.

In his book *The 500 Greatest Singles Since Punk And Disco*, Garry Mulholland writes: "It really was a completely new sound, and an announcement of new possibilities…It showed everyone a place that the new music could travel to. Unfortunately that turned out to be, in many cases, to be a place called goth."

Ah well, it was good while it lasted.

HONG KONG GARDEN / VOICES SINGLE. POLYDOR. 1978

"I was very lonely actually. The few friends I had were gypsies. When I was eight I tried to commit suicide to get noticed by my parents. I used to do things like fall on the floor upstairs so that they'd think I'd fallen downstairs, and I'd have bottles of pills in my hands. I've always felt on the outside, really."

Siouxsie Sioux talking to the *New Musical Express*'s Paul Morley, 1978

Siouxsie Sioux was so cool she could get away with horizontal AND vertical stripes.

Skin Disease

I'm Thick

And punk begat Oi! Oi was back-to-basics, no-nonsense, working-class punk rock for blokes who liked a pint and a laugh. It was profoundly anti-intellectual and passionately apolitical. Unfortunately, not giving a toss about politics also meant putting up with all the nazi skinheads who came to the Oi shows. The vast majority of the Oi bands were not nazis but the scene was plagued from day one by fans who were.

In his autobiography *Footnote*, Boff Whalley of anarchist punkers Chumbawamba (who later, amazingly, had a massive worldwide hit with the single "Tubthumping") writes sneeringly that Oi was "dodgy, badly produced skinhead music" with "crypto fascist overtones" and a "dumbed-down gang mentality".

Boff and a couple of mates recorded a couple of spoof Oi songs and sent them to Garry Bushell, the London-based music journalist who was Oi's biggest champion. Bushell loved the songs and invited the non-existent Skin Disease to record a track for a forthcoming Oi EP. Dressed up as skinheads, the anarchists duly turned up at the recording studio and started playing their "new" song "I'm Thick", the lyrics of which were "I'm thick" repeated over and over again. The producers of the EP were two members of the London Oi band The Cockney Rejects. They were more than a little confused.

"Is that it?"

"That's it."

"What, nuffing else?"

"No, that's it."

Bog picks up the story: "Several months later 'I'm Thick' by Skin Disease appeared on the *Back On The Streets* EP alongside songs glorifying violence, ignorance and the British army's victory in the Falklands war."

And that's the end of the story.

"What, nuffing else?"

No, that's it.

BACK ON THE STREETS EP. SECRET. 1982

The Slits

Typical Girls

The Slits are the classic example of the can't-play-must-play punk band. When they started they really didn't know one end of a guitar from another, and on their first tour Mick Jones from The Clash had to tune their instruments for them. This was happening a lot in 1976 and 1977. You just got on stage and did it – how hard could it be? And if you made a dreadful racket, so what? You had the rest of your life to learn how to play your guitar properly (if you could be bothered). In the meantime, what were you going to do? Take lessons? Or just get up there and DO IT!

The Slits formed in 1976 when Palmolive (later to drum for The Raincoats) approached a crazy-haired German woman called Ari Up at a Patti Smith gig. The new group achieved a kind of shambling notoriety when they opened for The Clash on their 1977 White Riot tour of the UK. But The Slits knew what thousands of other punk kids were learning – that not knowing how to play music properly freed you up to make a new music.

Visually The Slits were stunning. They looked like a punk version of *The Wild Women Of Wonga*. Dreadlocked singer Ari Up wore underwear outside her clothes – men's underwear. The Slits were variously described as a "Rasta-feminist freak show" and the "All Girl Punk Horror". Like the good punks they were, The Slits took the girly-girl image of the typical female pop/rock star and slashed it to ribbons.

In 1979 The Slits teamed up with veteran reggae producer Dennis Bovell, and together they made some fantastic music.

Ari Up of The Slits – punk's first supermodel.

"Typical Girls" is a breathlessly skippy, dub-tinged song in which The Slits parody the Stepford Wife conformity of the un-punked female stereotype: "Don't create, don't rebel...Typical girls/ Worry about spots, and fat, and natural smells."

This is punk feminism at its sardonic best. A decade and a half later The Slits would be rediscovered by a new generation of pissed-off female punks – the Riot Grrls.

File between Patti Smith's "Radio Ethiopia" and Huggy Bear's "Her Jazz". This is the history of rock music that you've not been taught.

> # "The Slits are both a superb illustration of how punk was so much more than testeronic mock-metal and a textbook example of the regularly forgotten truth that, in rock music, imagination is to technical ability as 857 billion is to minus 10."
>
> **Steven Wells, *New Musical Express***

TYPICAL GIRLS / I HEARD IT THROUGH THE GRAPEVINE SINGLE. ISLAND. 1979

Social Distortion
Mommy's Little Monster

Writing about these songs in alphabetical order is a total mindfuck. One minute we're talking about spidery punk-dub experiments in rainy west London in 1979, and then suddenly SREEEEEEEEEEE we fast forward to the thudding drums and screaming guitars of 1980s back-to-basics hardcore in sunny Orange County California. Have we gone backwards or have we gone forwards?

Both. By the 1980s punk was out of control. What had once been restricted to a few clubs in New York and London was now re-exploding all over the place. And it wasn't following anybody's punk rules. Kids were reinventing punk in their own image (and if you don't like it, granddad, tough). But don't worry – these new kids would be considered old hat in a couple of months' time, rendered obsolete by yet another generation of spiky young gobshites. By 1982 the truly global nature of the punk scene meant that it was impossible for anyone individual to keep tabs on what was going on – and remain sane.

So here we are in southern California. Most of the punks here come from homes with refrigerators that are bigger than most English houses (OK, so we exaggerate slightly). But poverty is relative, and the suburban kids of LA and its environs are living in a sterilized Disneyland. This is the American Dream and, say the punks, it sucks.

Social Distortion were an amazing live band and their brilliant 1982 album, *Mommy's Little Monster*, had a massive impact on all the US punk bands that followed. The title track is a ferocious and witty portrayal of middle-class kiddies gone rotten. "Mommy's little monster shoots methadrine/ Mommy's little monster had sex at fifteen," roars singer Mike Ness. Here, Ness is drawing on his own life story. Ness himself left home at 15 and spent years fucked up on drugs and/or in jail.

The radical hippies of the 1960s had urged American children to "kill your parents". The punks went one better than this. They revenged themselves on the society that fucked them up by becoming their parents' worst nightmare.

America was about to slip into the conformist, suit-wearing, flag-waving, ass-kissing, corporate hell of the Reagan years. But hardcore bands like Social Distortion – singing about the fucked-up state of American society in general and the fucked-up American family in particular – were going to fight them all the way. Hardcore would help keep the real American dream – the one about freedom of expression and unbridled creativity – alive while all around them their fellow citizens turned into blinkered Reaganite pod-people. Punk was about to go underground – and there it would thrive and flourish.

For the sleeve notes to Social Distortion's 1989 album *Live At The Roxy*, Mike Ness wrote: "As a song writer, I am a reactionary. Everything I write about is in reaction to life around me. This song is the result of growing up the way that I wanted to, not the way I was told I had to. Back in 1982 when I wrote the song, the media was calling us a menace to society, us punk rockers. They were telling us we couldn't play this kind of music and that we couldn't look the way that we did and that the movement was going to die. We told them over our dead bodies. This song represents a dissatisfaction about the way things were. And you know what? We're still not satisfied."

MOMMY'S LITTLE MONSTER ALBUM. 13TH FLOOR. 1983

Stiff Little Fingers
Alternative Ulster

The English punks might have thought the Californian punks had it easy (what with their house-sized refrigerators and all that) but they should have tried being a punk in the northern Irish city of Belfast.

In the 1920s Ireland finally won its independence from the British Empire – but there was a catch. Northern Ireland, the area around the city of Belfast, was predominantly populated by Protestants who were fiercely loyal to Britain. And so a compromise was reached. Most of Ireland would be given its independence but the north, including Belfast, would remain British.

In the late 1960s the Catholic minority in Northern Ireland started demanding equal treatment and an end to discrimination. The police responded by beating the crap out of them. Protestant mobs – often led by armed police – attacked Catholic areas. Soon the situation got so bad that the British army were sent in, but this made things even worse. For the next three decades the people of Northern Ireland (already one of the poorest and most depressed areas in Europe) suffered not only armed occupation but also the bombing and shooting campaigns of both Protestant and Catholic terrorists.

Stiff Little Fingers were Northern Ireland's biggest punk band. You think you've got it tough, punk? These kids grew up with armoured cars patrolling the streets. The Fingers looked like The Clash, sang about "the troubles" and were viewed with suspicion by both Catholics and Protestants. In fact there were kids from both Catholic and Protestant backgrounds in the band, but that was irrelevant. Stiff Little Fingers were punks. They were pissed off. And they rocked.

Perhaps surprisingly, the punks in mainland Britain had very little to say about the ongoing war that was happening just on their doorstep. The Gang Of Four had written the brilliant "Armalite Rifle", Sham 69 had offered up the truly dumb and dreadful "Belfast Boy" and the Angelic Upstarts had composed the mournful "Last Night Another Soldier". But that was about it. So when London

STIFF LITTLE FINGERS
TURBOSOUND
Pearl
STIFF LITTLE FINGERS
Marshall

Stiff Little Fingers' Jake Burns is hoisted aloft by giant digits.

Suspect Device

punk heroes The Clash came over and had their photos taken looking mean and tough in front of the barbed wire and the barricades, most people in Belfast thought it was a bloody cheek.

But in the shape of Stiff Little Fingers, Northern Ireland at last had a band that could write about what it was like growing up in a war zone from first-hand experience.

"Alternative Ulster" – a great song – was written at the request of a local punk journalist who had a fanzine of the same name. The idea was that the song would be made into a flexi-disc to be given away with the fanzine. "But he thought it was fucking shit," remembers Stiff Little Fingers' guitarist Jake Burns.

Later that same fanzine journalist would get a job on the then punk-obsessed London music paper *New Musical Express*. One of the first articles he wrote for the *NME* was an interview with Stiff Little Fingers in which he crucified the band for being self-glorifying punk-lite fakes. Oh dear. The odd thing is that nobody now remembers that journalist's name, while the song he dismissed as "shit" is now widely regarded as an all-time punk classic. Ha!

"A lot of people make grandiose claims for the song. They see it as either a republican [Catholic] or loyalist [Protestant] rallying call," says Jake. "It was nothing to do with that at all. It was just about everyday life in Belfast. And this might sound strange, seeing as it was a city being torn apart by riots and bombings, but Belfast was actually a really fucking boring place to be. They locked the security-gates around the city at six o'clock so there was nowhere to go. And no bands would come and play because they couldn't get the insurance. That happened to The Clash – they turned up and were told they couldn't play. So we rioted. Because that was what you did in Belfast."

"Suspect Device" was army and police jargon for a car or an abandoned bag that might possibly contain a bomb. There were a lot of suspect devices on the streets of Belfast in the 1970s.

In the Stiff Little Fingers' early days, Jake had met up with a couple of punk-enthused local journalists to try to get the band some publicity. "At that time we were playing a rag-bag of Damned, Clash and Sex Pistols covers," remembers Jake.

The journalists encouraged Jake to write songs about growing up and living in Belfast. And then one of them, Gordon Ogilvie, reached into his pocket and handed over the finished lyric of "Suspect Device".

"I was completely blown away by it" says Jake (no pun intended).

INFLAMMABLE MATERIAL ALBUM. RIGID DIGITS/ROUGH TRADE. 1978

The Stranglers

Peaches

The Stranglers had been around since before the Sex Pistols. They were a menacing, lairy, macho band, more than capable of flights of intellectual erudition but usually choosing to portray themselves as horrible, leering sexist thugs instead.

So The Stranglers weren't "real" punk and they were far from PC, but none of that mattered in the end because they played great punk rock.

"Peaches" is a disgraceful record. It really is. The lyrics consist of singer Hugh Cornwell growling lustily after passing bikini-clad females, but what made the song so irresistible was incredibly handsome Jean-Jacques Burnell's thundering bass riff. Surly JJ (as he was known) had a black belt in karate and he also made the bass guitar (usually considered a Cinderella instrument) sexy and cool.

It's a great record. But utterly indefensible, of course. Tut tut.

No More Heroes

The Stranglers might have been too old (and too sexist) to be considered proper punks but they had an amazing talent for writing blindingly pertinent punk anthems. Years later a socialist skinhead/punk band called The Redskins would come up with the lyrics "Take no heroes/ Only inspiration" but The Stranglers beat them to it.

"Heroes" is a clever lyric. On the one hand it seems to be bemoaning the fact that the old Victorian idea of the historical hero – the "great men" who single-handedly changed the world – had gone out of fashion. But it was also, on another level, echoing the punk idea that you became your own hero. The previous generation of rockers had idolized their guitar heroes. Kids at Eric Clapton concerts would hold up banners saying "CLAPTON IS GOD!" And they meant it. But the basic message of punk was that the kid in the crowd was in every way the equal of the kid on the stage.

On yet another level the song seems to be implying that there are "no more heroes" anymore – apart from, of course, The Stranglers themselves. This was typical of the air of swaggering macho arrogance that The Stranglers worked so hard to maintain (and that pissed so many people off).

Cornwell sings about Leon Trotsky "who got an icepick that made his ears burn". Leon Trotsky had been one of the leaders of the Bolshevik Party that had led the communist Russian Revolution in 1917. When Josef Stalin took control of the Soviet Union, Trotsky fled abroad. In 1940 he was murdered in Mexico – stabbed in the head with an icepick – by an assassin following Stalin's orders.

Trotsky was a big hero for many of the people on the British left at the time – particularly members of the Socialist Workers Party, which had been instrumental in helping to set up Rock Against Racism. The Stranglers loved annoying people – they lived for it. Yet another reason why they are now considered to be a punk band.

Something Better Change

"Something Better Change" was written by mean, moody and incredibly sexy bassist JJ Burnell (who once described himself as "a left-wing fascist"). It brilliantly sums up both the punk 'tude and the general feeling of revolution that was in the air in 1977.

Looking back now it is hard to pinpoint why punk happened, why so much energy was released in such a short space of time, why so many people seemed ready and able to overturn the old musical order and replace it with something fresher and more vital. But change was definitely in the air, and this song captures that feeling of accelerating revolt and rebellion brilliantly.

"The Stranglers (were) ghastly, retro rubbish."

Jon Savage, *3AM* magazine

Svelte, sophisticated and sexist – JJ Burnell of The Stranglers.

"Punk was wild, outcast, vicious and protective at the same time. It wasn't boring, and it wasn't straight (I don't mean this just in terms of sexuality, but in a perceptual sense). It did not, initially, reinforce the dominant values. So if you're pissed off, you might pick up some tips. You might find a bunch of outcasts coming together curiously uplifting."

Jon Savage, *3AM* magazine

PEACHES / GO BUDDY GO
SINGLE. UNITED ARTISTS. 1977

SOMETHING BETTER CHANGE /
STRAIGHTEN OUT
SINGLE. UNITED ARTISTS. 1977

NO MORE HEROES /
IN THE SHADOWS
SINGLE. UNITED ARTISTS. 1977

Talking Heads

Psycho Killer

The barrier between "high art" and "popular culture" was one of the many that punk tried to rip down and nobody did it more effectively than New York's Talking Heads.

Talking Heads, like Blondie, were one of the New York bands who emerged in 1976 and 1977 thinking that they were playing pop. This was true, they were, but in the case of Talking Heads they were making music that sounded like pop music from three years down the line. The stuff they recorded in 1977 was uncannily similar to the music that would be made in the early '80s by pop bands that had been exposed to and radically changed by punk. By that time, of course, Talking Heads had moved even further ahead.

Talking Heads.

Talking Heads are one of the bands most often quoted by those wishing to illustrate the fact that there was much, much more to punk than jack-hammered guitars, socio-political ranting and spitting. The Heads were caught between two stools. They wanted to make art and they wanted to make pop – and I think that's as good a definition of punk as you're ever likely to hear.

Singer David Byrne had a quiet, unassuming manner and the disturbing habit of twitching (rather like the lunatic killer played by Anthony Perkins in the movie *Psycho*). This is used to great effect on 1979's "mutant disco" hit, "Psycho Killer".

Byrne looks and sings like a librarian (think Giles out of *Buffy The Vampire Slayer*, except with a middle-class American accent and madly staring eyes). As the hysteria in Byrne's voice mounts, he starts to babble in French. The "psycho killer" is closer than you think (and I'm only guessing, but I think it's probably Dave himself). When he warns us to "run, run, run away", that's the time to start backing towards the door while smiling and scanning the room for sharp-edged objects with your peripheral vision.

David Byrne and Tina Weymouth.

"Psycho Killer" is a spookier second cousin to The Adverts' "Gary Gilmore's Eyes". It bears pretty much the same relationship to The Damned's horror-punk offerings as a slickly made, modern psychological thriller does to *Abbot & Costello Meet Dracula*.

" 'Psycho Killer' was written as an exercise with someone else's approach in mind," remembers Byrne. "I had been listening to Alice Cooper – *Billion Dollar Babies*, I think – and I thought it was really funny stuff. I thought, 'Hey, I can do this!' It was sort of an experiment to see if I could write something.

"I thought I would write a song about a very dramatic subject the way [Alice Cooper] does, but from inside the person, playing down the drama. Rather than making it theatrical the way Alice Cooper would, I'd go for what's going on inside the killer's mind, what I imagined he might be thinking.

"I wanted it to be like Randy Newman doing Alice Cooper. One way of telling the story would be to describe everything that happens – 'he walks across the room, he takes so many steps, he's wearing such-and-such.' That tells you everything that's going on, on one level, but it doesn't involve you emotionally. The other extreme is to describe it all as a series of sensations. I think that sometimes has more power and affects people a little stronger. It seemed a natural delusion that a psychotic killer would imagine himself as very refined and use a foreign language to talk to himself."

"I hate people when they're not polite..."

**TALKING HEADS 77
ALBUM. SIRE. 1977**

Television

Marquee Moon

Television were one of the key players in the confused, chaotic, incestuous and incredibly vibrant New York punk scene of 1974 to 1976.

The New York scene had something the London bands would never have. London was an old city – the former capital of a dead empire. London attracted millions of tourists who treated the place like a walk-in museum.

New York was the future happening right now. It was the capital city of the newly emergent superduperpower. And, like Rome in its imperial heyday, New York was synonymous with sleaze, aggression, sex and decadence. This was the New York of Martin Scorcese's *Taxi Driver*. The place where anything could and would happen – and at twice the speed of anywhere else. New York was punk rock – sculpted in glass, steel, brick and concrete.

So imagine how totally pissed off the NY punks were when the Sex Pistols stole their crown. I once stayed overnight in the apartment of some NY punkers. When they thought I'd gone to sleep they started bitching. I could hear every word through the paper-thin walls: "Those snooty, stuck-up fuckin' tea-sipping sons-of-fuckin'-bitches think they fuckin' invented punk!"

For the record, this is one "tea bag" who is willing to admit that we didn't. America did. New York did. Television did. OK?

Television's 1977 *Marquee Moon* album surprised everybody. While their contemporaries were all speeding up and getting louder, Television (the band that had once been fronted by devil-dog Richard Hell) out-punked everyone by mellowing the fuck out.

Marquee Moon was years ahead of its time – a foretaste of the way British punk bands like Siouxsie And The Banshees would start experimenting with a more minimalist and angular sound two years later. *Marquee Moon* is now recognized as one of the great punk albums – a recording that looked to the possibilities of punk at a time when most punk bands were still throwing their rattles out of their prams and screaming their spiky heads off.

Television with, er, a television.

Lyrically the title track is a ramble through rock'n'roll Americana – similar to Patti Smith's "Piss Factory" but less vitriolic – but it's the incredible guitar interplay that makes "Marquee Moon" one of those punk records that are loved even by people who claim to hate punk.

It was too much too soon, but "Marquee Moon" would be eagerly revisited by the new punks (once the shouting had died down).

MARQUEE MOON ALBUM. ELEKTRA RECORDS. 1977

Television Personalities

Part Time Punks

Like The Members' "Sound Of The Suburbs", "Part Time Punks" is British punk rock taking a good, hard look at itself – and then laughing like a drain.

The first punk show I ever went to was The Adverts and The Damned. I had pinned my flared jeans back with safety pins and attempted to spike my unruly hair with soap. The older punks started at me with a mixture of pity and contempt. On the way out of the gig I stopped a policeman and asked where the nearest telephone box was.

"Why?" snarled the copper suspiciously.

"Because I've got to phone my mum to let her know I'm going to be home late," I replied.

Yes, folks, I admit it – I WAS a part-time punk.

1977 was an incredibly pretentious time. Everybody was pretending to be something they weren't. That was (is) the whole point of punk. Do you think Johnny Rotten was born with shit teeth, madly staring eyes and the posture of a demented hunchback? And as punk spread into the suburbs and started attracting every geek, nerd, knobhead and nebbish (me included), the gap between the wannabe reality and the image of the sussed, street-wise and battle-hardened urban punk rocker grew wider and wider.

The Television Personalities jumped into that gap with both feet. With this rinky-dinky DIY punk classic, they ripped the royal piss out of us – and we loved it, because it was pretty damn obvious that the TVPs were part-time punks themselves. I mean, who the hell would want to be a full-time punk? Spitting beer all over your mum during Sunday lunch, telling your teacher to "fuck off" because he was a "boring old fart" and going home at night to sleep in black leather bondage pyjamas worn over a Seditionaries "wanking cowboys" T-shirt? I mean, it's just not practical, is it?

> **"The TVPs were around at the dawn of punk, well actually the breakfast to be more accurate. . ."**
>
> **Television Personalities biog, Damaged Goods website**

WHERE'S BILL GRUNDY NOW? EP. KING'S ROAD. 1978

The Undertones

Teenage Kicks

If there is any record that can make a grown punk cry, it is "Teenage Kicks" by The Undertones.

The Undertones were a bunch of scruffy urchins who played Ramones/Buzzcocks-style pop punk in the Northern Ireland city of Derry. And they had in singer Feargal Sharkey a young man possessed of the voice of an angel and the face of a gargoyle.

The Undertones' first single, "Teenage Kicks", is quite possibly the best pop-punk song ever. The influential John Peel – whose BBC radio show had been a crucial part of the UK punk explosion – argues to this day that it is quite simply the greatest pop song – of any genre – ever recorded.

"There's nothing you could add to it or subtract from it that would improve it," says Peel. "Even now it reduces me to tears every time I hear it."

It is a throbbing, urgent record, but the lyrics, apparently about the fluffy innocence of first-time love, are in fact about a far seedier subject.

"The original chorus was 'I want to hold it – hold it tight – get Teenage Kicks right through the night'," says Feargal Sharkey. "It was about a male Catholic boy in Ireland wanking [masturbating] 'cos he couldn't get off with anybody."

"The Ramones weren't writing about the Northern Ireland troubles so we decided 'Well, I don't think we will either'."

Michael Bradley, Undertones bassist

TEENAGE KICKS
SINGLE. SIRE. 1978

Wire
12XU

One of the most influential albums of 1977 was *Live At The Roxy*. The Roxy was a London punk club, not unlike New York's CBGB. Every night weird and wonderful punk acts, some only formed that afternoon, would take to the stage and try to play their instruments. In musical terms *Live At The Roxy* was as rough as a burglar's dog, but one track does stand out – "12XU" by Wire. Amid the slapstick and the chaos, Wire were fumbling their way towards a short, sharp and incredibly tense minimalist rock. Ears pricked up. This was something different.

By the time Wire recorded their debut album, *Pink Flag*, they'd nailed the sound down. This was punk stripped down to its bones, the exact opposite of the Sex Pistols' "more is more" approach. Wire were lean, mean and, well, wiry. They called their music "dugga" – after the "dugga-dugga" bass lines – and what seemed radical at the time soon became a punk staple (check out the first Elastica album, for instance).

The stand-out track was "12XU". The lyrics, in their entirety, were: "Saw you in a mag kissing a man, I got you in a corner got you in a corner, 12xU." When the lines were repeated "mag" became "fag" and "corner" became "cottage" ("cottaging" being gay slang for the solicitation of sex in a public toilet). "In a way it's a gay song," explained bassist Graham Lewis, "and in another it isn't. It's what anyone wants to take out of it."

"It's about sexual exertion in any direction, really," added guitarist Bruce Gilbert.

The X in the line "12XU" stands for "fuck". "It was a joke about censoring," explained vocalist Colin Newman. "Lots of people were putting out records with 'Fuck' on them and immediately getting banned."

PINK FLAG
ALBUM. HARVEST. 1977

Voice of an angel, face of a gargoyle – The Undertones' Feargal Sharkey.

X-Ray Spex
Oh Bondage Up Yours!

Wire's "12XU" might have caused a stir, but the truly outstanding track on the now legendary *Live At The Roxy* album was "Oh Bondage Up Yours!" by X-Ray Spex.

The track starts with the shy, timid – almost disembodied – voice of a small girl saying: "Some people think little girls should be seen and not heard. But I say…[and now comes a full-throated Amazon roar] OH BONDAGE, UP YOURS! 1,2,3,4!"

There then follows an amateurishly clumsy drum roll, a blast of barely competent and obviously out-of-tune saxophone and the female singer half sings and half yells the most amazing lyric – full of images taken straight from the Marquis de Sade's most fevered sado-masochistic nightmares. The singers asks to be beaten, tied up, chained to a wall and flayed. And each burst ends with the same declamation – "OH BONDAGE, UP YOURS!"

The first time I heard "Bondage" I felt electricity spark down the full length of my spine. This wasn't music designed to stimulate the frontal lobes (although it did that, too); this was junk food for the reptile brain stem. This was rock'n'roll that went straight for the sex organs. This was music that made you want to go "AAAAAAAARGH!"

Marion Elliot was born of a Somali father and an English mother. She worked in the fashion industry and had a brief career as a "lover's rock" pop-reggae singer. On her 19th birthday she saw the Sex Pistols.

She put an ad in the London music paper *Melody Maker*: "Young punx who want to stick it together." She changed her name to Poly Styrene and she started writing songs.

"My thing was more like consumerism, plastic, artificial living," she explains in Jon Savage's *England's Dreaming*. "There was so much junk then. The idea was to send it all up. Screaming about it, saying – Look, this is what you have done to me, turned me into this piece of styrofoam. I am your product. And this is what you have created; do you like her?

"One of the first songs we did was 'Oh Bondage Up Yours!' It was about being in bondage to material life. In other words it was a call for liberation. It was saying: 'Bondage? – forget it! I am not going to be bound by the laws of consumerism or bound by my own senses.' It has that line in it: 'Chain smoke, chain gang, I consume you all'; you are tied to these activities for somebody else's profit."

The Day The World Turned Day-Glo

Poly had formerly been a bit of a nature-loving hippie chick. This gave her lyrics an extra edge but they also dovetailed beautifully into punk's cheap, trashy, primary-coloured plastic aesthetic. X-Ray Spex were a miraculous combination – a bubblegum pop band with a brilliant socio-political critique of modern society.

Although now often overlooked by those who think 1977 Brit punk started and finished with the Sex Pistols and The Clash, X-Ray Spex were actually one of the most musically accomplished of the "original" punks (once they'd learned to play their instruments – a bit). And lyrically nobody could touch them.

"Day-Glo" is an amazing account of a nightmare world where everything is made from brightly coloured plastic, and all of nature has been paved in styrofoam and painted in brain-frying shocking pinks and pastel blues. It's as if the dystopian horror-world of *1984* or *Terminator* has been redesigned to suit the aesthetic sensibilities of a sugar-spiked two-year-old child. Someone once described Poly Styrene's imaginative landscape as being like that of Radiohead – if Thom Yorke had been force-fed so many hallucinogenic drugs that his brains dribbled out of his ears. That someone was me. And I was right.

Germ Free Adolescence

If punk was about anything, it was about perversity. That's why perfectly sensible young men renamed themselves Johnny Rotten or Rat Scabies. That's why fresh-faced young girls dressed themselves up in garbage bags and wore enough make-up to paint every whore in Paris for a year. And that's why I wore a home-made "Vomit On The Aged" badge to my first Clash gig.

All the clichés of punk – the dog collar, the ripped T-shirts, the safety pins and the garbage bags – were comments on the stupidity and futility of mindless consumerism. Punk turned consumerism on its head. If you hadn't made your own clothes, or found them in skips, garbage cans or in thrift shops, then you really weren't trying.

In 1978 Boff Whalley – later to become a member of the anarchist punk band Chumbawamba – was a teenage punk in the northern English town of Burnley. "I was wearing one of those cream cotton holiday jackets that old blokes wear on blustery seafronts on the English south coast, " he recalls in his autobiography *Footnotes*. "I'd bought it second hand and stencilled GRANDAD'S HOLIDAY COAT across the front. Black drainpipe trousers, eight-hole Doctor Marten boots. Hair stuck up, big grin, T-shirt which read – 'I Don't Want To Go To Art School'.

"It's true, I did look like a cunt. The *precise* reason for spending so long with a stencil set and a sewing machine. If they could have charged me with *looking like a cunt* or even with *intent to look like a cunt*...I would have been very pleased..."

No other band explored this perversity as thoroughly or as well as X-Ray Spex. Their music was high satire. It took the shiny, gleaming, perfect world offered by the advertising industry and turned up the focus, the contrast, the brightness, the colours and the volume.

George Orwell (the English novelist who wrote the political satires *1984* and *Animal Farm*) once described the advertising industry as "rattling the stick in the pig-trough of capitalism".

X-Ray Spex drank deep at this trough. They became super-consumers and they spewed capitalism's useless shit right back in its face.

It's this world of gleamingly clean and absolutely brain-dead perfection that is explored in "Germ Free Adolescence". The youth in the song is the ad-industry's dream. He/she is super-clean – perfect teeth, perfect hair, perfect nails. And the glazed eyes of a walking corpse.

The talented and slightly demented Poly Styrene of X-Ray Spex.

Punk said that you were defined not by what you consumed but by what you did, by what you *created*. And nobody said it better than X-Ray Spex.

OH BONDAGE UP YOURS / I AM A CLICHÉ SINGLE. VIRGIN. 1977

GERM FREE ADOLESCENTS. ALBUM. EMI. 1978

Index